QUEER VIRTUE

QUEER VIRTUE

What LGBTQ People Know About Life and Love and How It Can Revitalize Christianity

The Reverend Elizabeth M. Edman

QUEER ACTION/QUEER IDEAS
A Series Edited by Michael Bronski

Beacon Press
Boston

BEACON PRESS
Boston, Massachusetts
www.beacon.org

Beacon Press books
are published under the auspices of
the Unitarian Universalist Association of Congregations.

19 18 17 16   8 7 6 5 4 3 2 1

This book is printed on acid-free paper that meets the uncoated paper
ANSI/NISO specifications for permanence as revised in 1992.

Text design and composition by Wilsted & Taylor Publishing Services

Queer Ideas—a unique series addressing
pivotal issues within the LGBT movement

LIBRARY OF CONGRESS CATALOGING-IN-PUBLICATION DATA

Names: Edman, Elizabeth M.
Title: Queer virtue : what LGBTQ people know about life and love and how it
    can revitalize Christianity / The Reverend Elizabeth M. Edman.
Description: Boston : Beacon Press, 2016. | Series: Queer action/queer ideas
    | Includes bibliographical references.
Identifiers: LCCN 2015027701 | ISBN 978-0-8070-6134-3 (hardcover : alk.
    paper) | ISBN 978-0-8070-6135-0 (ebook)
Subjects: LCSH: Queer theology. | Sex—Religious aspects—Christianity. |
    Queer theory. | Christianity.
Classification: LCC BT83.65.E36 2016 | DDC 230.086/64—dc23 LC record
    available at http://lccn.loc.gov/2015027701

For Michael+

that suffering which I showed unto thee
and the rest in the dance,
I will that it be called a mystery.

CONTENTS

A NOTE FROM THE SERIES EDITOR

The words "queer" and "virtue" hardly ever appear together. Like alpha and omega, sin and grace, and wrong and right, they are always seen as opposing ends of a spectrum. Elizabeth Edman's *Queer Virtue: What LGBTQ People Know About Life and Love and How It Can Revitalize Christianity* brilliantly, succinctly, and with enormous empathy and insight argues that these terms, far from being oppositional, are wedded in ways that make them distinctly unique. Indeed, brought together they are the quintessence of Christianity.

The last four decades, since the advent of Gay Liberation in 1969, have produced a wealth of literature dealing with the troubled, ever-evolving relationship between feminism, (homo)sexuality, and Christianity: Mary Daly's revolutionary *Beyond God the Father: Toward a Philosophy of Women's Liberation* (1973), John Boswell's *Christianity, Social Tolerance, and Homosexuality: Gay People in Western Europe from the Beginning of the Christian Era to the Fourteenth Century* (1980), Mark D. Jordan's *The Invention of Sodomy in Christian Theology* (1997), and Patrick S. Cheng's *From Sin to Amazing Grace: Discovering the Queer Christ* (2012) all gave us fresh ways to think about how historically and theologically the relationship between Christianity and queerness is far more complex than we had ever imagined. *Queer Virtue* builds on these works and takes them a step further—if modern Christianity is in a crisis, it can be saved, revitalized, by the contemporary queer experience and consciousness. Edman's vision challenges and reawakens Christianity from the inside and forces believers and nonbelievers alike to rethink and reanimate their long held assumptions.

We live in a country in which the lived experience of being LGBTQ and the internal experience and practice of being Christian seem to continually clash: same-sex marriage debates, religious freedom exemptions, the implications of antigay sentiments, and the limits of hate crime laws are in the headlines every day. *Queer Virtue* addresses none of this directly—and yet, with theological and political perceptivity, Edman gives us new ways to think about all of these issues by demanding that we understand queerness not as compatible with Christianity, but an embodiment of it.

MICHAEL BRONSKI
Series Editor, Queer Action/Queer Ideas

AUTHOR'S NOTE

This book is born of three decades of studying, preaching, and teaching from the western canon of Christian scripture. This canon includes the Hebrew/Jewish scriptures that were sacred texts for Jesus, Paul, and the communities that Paul founded; the four synoptic Gospels; the Acts of the Apostles; numerous epistles including those attributed to Paul; the book of Revelation; and for some denominations, the books of the Apocrypha. Therefore, when I use the term "Christianity" in this book, I refer to those strands of the Christian tradition whose traditional sacred texts are those of the Western canon. My understanding of what constitutes core theology in this Western tradition is informed by the work of the councils of the fourth through the ninth centuries CE. By "Christian," I thus include Roman Catholicism, Anglicanism, other Protestant denominations often referred to in the United States as "mainline" (Lutherans, Methodists, Presbyterians, etc.), and evangelical Protestantism. I would also include progressive faith communities such as the Unitarian Universalists and Quakers to the extent that such communities or members consider themselves Christian.

There are thus many strains of Christianity that are not included in my scope, including Eastern Orthodoxy and esoteric strains of Christianity such as Gnosticism. In some ways I suspect that these traditions are able to embrace the liminality of the sacred with greater ease than Western Christianity; however, lacking expertise in these traditions, I leave it to others to discuss whether they can be described as inherently queer.

Of those Christian traditions that fall within my scope, all are global movements, and I offer the ideas in this book for consideration by their full global communities. My intention here is not to universalize a single, decisive interpretation of Christianity and impose it on people who live in contexts and experience modes of worship very different from what I experience as an American of European descent. With love and respect, I thus defer to my Christian siblings across the globe to articulate how the queerness of our tradition is manifest for them, undoubtedly in ways that I have not yet comprehended.

I occasionally refer broadly to "the church." This term refers to the global community of faith, characterized in the Nicene Creed as "one holy catholic and apostolic." Within this "church" there is considerable breadth of opinion about issues raised in this book. Therefore it matters to underscore this point: there are many Christian denominations that now recognize the inherent worth of LGBTQ people. Several denominations have long been prophetic on this front, including the United Church of Christ, Unitarian Universalists, Quakers, and my own Episcopal Church. The Metropolitan Community Church has been positively heroic in its proclamation of a queer-positive gospel. I hold in highest regard the countless clergy and laypeople, queer and nonqueer, who over the past fifty years have promoted LGBTQ justice in Christian churches globally. Many LGBTQ clergy are now bringing their queerly attuned gifts to bear in ways that invigorate congregations graced by their leadership. Thus I acknowledge with respect and gratitude the existence of queer-positive individuals and denominations even as I write about homophobic strains of Christianity; and I do not in any way mean to imply that Christianity is universally homophobic when I write that many homophobic enterprises call themselves Christian.

One term that I use is "nominal Christianity." By this I simply mean "people and communities who call themselves Christian," regardless of where those individual people or churches land on the ideological spectrum. "Nominal Christianity" is not meant to be a disparaging term in itself, but a simple and neutral way to say "that's who they say they are." When I talk about "authentic Christianity," I am referring to a lived faith in keeping with the ancient tradition that has been handed down in the Western canon of scripture and from the early (especially pre-sixth-century) church. "In keeping with the ancient tradition" is of course quite a broad description. None of our communities lives it perfectly, and there are aspects of this tradition that a socially conservative congregation might live more "authentically" than a socially progressive one. I will therefore focus tightly on one specific aspect of "authentic Christianity" as a spiritual journey that prioritizes the ancient Christian impulse to rupture simplistic binaries, especially those pertaining to the relationship between Self and Other.

A WORD ABOUT PRONOUN USAGE IN THIS BOOK

Gender binaries remain entrenched for English-speaking people because they are so firmly entrenched in our language. Lacking gender-neutral pronouns to refer to sentient beings, we are constantly asked to determine whether the person about whom we are speaking or writing is male or female. This creates a problem that is shared both by the church and by people who identify as LGBTQ.

Progressive liturgists have for decades grappled with the inadequacy of gender binaries in our speech about God, whom scripture tells us plainly is neither male nor female—or is both male and female—even as the text itself, in numerous tongues, continuously uses masculine language for God, somewhat offset by metaphors that confer female attributes both to God and to Jesus. LGBTQ people, meanwhile, find ourselves trying to create language that accurately communicates our complex relationships to gender identity.

This book will draw on queer linguistic insights as a genuine effort to speak as authentically as possible about the nature of God and humanity.

When speaking about God, I am going to employ gender-neutral pronouns developed by transgender activists and writers: "Ze" and "Hir." To clarify that I am referring to God, I will capitalize these words. When speaking about human beings, I will use a mix of "she/her," "ze/hir," and "he/him/his." I will choose one of these for each paragraph or example and attempt to use it consistently. I will also employ the term "trans*," asterisked, to acknowledge the diversity of gender identities and expressions that exist within transgender experience.

However you experience this usage—as jarring, joyful, comforting, impact-neutral, or something else—I invite you to dive in and, if it seems worthwhile, observe whatever is being revealed to you.

QUEER VIRTUE

INTRODUCTION

I am a queer priest.

By this, I mean so many things. Most obvious to others, I am a lesbian and I am a priest. Thus "queer" might indicate one of the particularities that I bring to my priesthood, in the same way one might say, "She is a woman priest," or, "He is a Nigerian priest."

This is true, but it is not enough. It is not nearly all that I mean.

For one thing, it elevates "priest" as noun above "queer," which is relegated to adjective. And in truth, "priest" just as clearly modifies "queer" in my soul. You see, I am also very much a priestly queer.

But that still doesn't capture what I mean.

As a priest, I am primarily concerned with the astonishing ways that God is constantly intruding on our lives, begging us to love and be loved, insinuating Hirself[1] in our hearts and minds, cracking us open, tearing us apart, rebuilding us, and keeping us alive throughout this terrifying, rigorous process. In theological circles, we refer to this as "the inbreaking of the Spirit." This transgressive nature of the sacred may not define the sacred—or it may—but it certainly is core to my experience of and devotion to the sacred. God ruptures our understanding of reality, constantly. God queers our lives and our world. It is fundamental to my priesthood to call attention to this queering, to name it for myself and others, to breathe life into our experience of it in preaching and in liturgy. I am thus a priest of the queer God who creates and calls us, ruptures and reconciles us, sustains and sanctifies us.

My lesbianism, my queerness, is part of who I am. It is built into my DNA as surely as my skin color, eye color, and the genetic kink that makes my hair curl. If I could choose to be gay, I would. I love

1

it in myself, so very much. But the question of choice aside, it is unquestionably part of me and for my entire life has informed my uptake of, well, everything.

My priestliness is part of who I am. Since I became conscious of myself and my desires, I have felt the inescapable draw of the sacred, the magic and mystery and power of something inside me, something bigger than me, something that connected me to other people, to life, to truth. My mother profoundly experienced God's transgressive power, and whatever made her so open to it, she passed on to me. She was a singer who experienced God most intimately through sacred music, so it was natural for her to enroll me and my sister and brother in the choir at our local Episcopal church as soon as we were big enough to stand and hold a hymnal. One gift of this was that from a very early age I participated in the leadership of our Sunday liturgies. It put me front and center, able to observe closely the mysterious goings-on at the altar. I was dazzled and captivated by the doings of our priest, at precisely the historical moment when our denomination was grappling with women's call to ordained ministry. I don't remember thinking consciously, "Hey, I can be a priest, too." I do remember the clear sense that, just as my mother's proper place in the church was in the loft, my proper place was at the altar.

These two components of my identity, these two markers, queer and priest, have always intertwined. To say that they have informed each other comes almost too close to suggesting that they are discrete. They are not divisible. And yet, they are distinct parts of who I am; they do mutually inform how I understand each of them; and they do inform how I understand everything else—God, the world, human life, and my own existence.

I am a queer priest. I am a priestly queer.

Both of these identity markers have informed my ethical development. My priesthood, rooted in the discipline of a spiritual path, tends to be explicit in its ethical demands. But the facts of queer life also unquestionably demand a lived ethical response. What may come as a surprise—what surprises me—is that the ethical demands placed on me by my identity as a queer person and by my involvement in the LGBTQ community tend to be far clearer and more rigorous than those placed on me by my ordination to holy orders.

Moreover, I have come to realize that queer ethical demands clearly and often exquisitely manifest widely recognized Christian virtues: spiritual discernment, rigorous self-assessment, honesty, courage, material risk, dedication to community life, and care for the marginalized and oppressed. I can't count how many times people have asked me how I reconcile my sexuality with my faith. The question always leaves me speechless, because I experience these two parts of my identity to be so deeply resonant with each other, particularly in terms of the kind of life they call me to live. I am convinced that this resonance says something important both about queerness and about Christianity.

For too long, public discourse about LGBTQ people has tended to operate from the premise that queer identity is morally problematic, but that there are specific instances of individual queer people who live upright lives. I argue precisely the opposite: while individual queer people struggle at times with moral failing—as all human beings do—in general I perceive queer identity to have at its core a moral center of high caliber, one that is both inspirational and aspirational. My experience being immersed in the lives and spiritual journeying of queer people tells me plainly not only that the divine is alive and well in us, but that many of us are deeply attuned to it.

Religious deprecation of queer people seems predicated on the idea that there is no spark of the divine in us—or that we possess such a spark but live in opposition to it, thus living in a state of perpetual sin. Either perspective ignores the alignment of ethical demands exacted by both Christian faith and queer life. In other words, that queer moral center, that spark, is not only *not* at odds with core tenets of Judeo-Christian belief, but is resonant with and in fact points to the most important, challenging, and vivifying aspects of the Judeo-Christian tradition.

I am not saying that queer people are or must be Christian. I am saying that authentic Christianity is and must be queer.

This is not to say that all Christians should become homosexual, or identify as LGBTQ—sexually queer. Rather, I mean "queer" as something that has at its center an impulse to disrupt any and all efforts to reduce into simplistic dualisms our experience of life, of God. Queer theory is historically rooted in the urgent need to

rupture, or disrupt, binary thinking about gender and sexual identity—and very specifically, to dismantle rigid attachment to male
and female as definitive poles.[2] This work is born of necessity for
queer people. We have had to carve out conceptual space for ourselves to inhabit—and not just conceptual, but also social, political,
and yes, theological.

Queering did not emerge as a relevant, important discourse
in the late twentieth century. Some of the most interesting historical queering has taken place in the church. Christian history
is salted with, has been flavored by, rich immersions into gender/
sexual queering, from Paul's encouragement to celibacy, to the
clerical dress/dresses—vestments—still worn today. Nor is queering an activity confined to gender and sexual expression, even in
the LGBTQ movement. Queering as an impulse and lens has been
applied to countless human perceptions and academic disciplines,
from architecture to biology to linguistics to theology. It is not a
stretch to see how Jesus ruptured simplistic dualisms all the time:
life and death, human and divine, sacred and profane. Paul's insistence that in Christ there is neither male nor female is the essence
of queering, set in the midst of a passage that also queers the lines
between Jew and Greek, slave and free.

These examples of queering are not marginal to Christian
tradition; they are core to our faith. I started this book because I
observed two things: first, my queer identity has taught me more
about how to be a good *Christian* than has the church. This is not
to say that my church experiences have been devoid of moral example. Throughout my life, I have often been astonished by the level
of faith and dedication to Christian community I have witnessed in
the lives of people I have known in the church: fellow parishioners,
priestly colleagues and mentors, my students in campus ministry.
What I am saying is that queer community has created a moral
code that I have internalized deeply, one which I have seen lived
out more consistently in queer community as community than I
have witnessed in the church as community. This living into ethical
demands in queer community has thus become a model for me, the
basis for virtuous aspiration, more effectively than has Christian life.

For any queer person, this may not come as a surprise. Our
status as members of a minority group dictates that ethical queer-

ness be lived out consciously with great regularity. That is, I am constantly having to make ethical decisions—personal, political, relational—that involve my queer identity. Perhaps because of this quotidian quality and the familiarity it breeds, I know and trust my queer ethical sensibility as much and at times even more than I know and trust the all-too-often-rarified world of Christian ethics. During times in my life when I have been most vigorously challenged, my queerness has provided a more reliable moral compass than my Christian faith. When I look back on the biggest mistakes I have made in my life, the clarity of my failing tends to stand out as a failure of my queer identity and obligations—even though, very often, there is a Christian imperative visibly at stake.

The second observation that got me writing is a question: If my queer identity informs my understanding of my Christian faith, might the lessons of queer identity help other Christians better understand their faith, too? I feel this question rear its head whenever I am part of discussions about addressing the spiritual needs of a particular group of people: gay people, survivors of intimate partner violence, people affected by HIV/AIDS, and others. In these discussions, I often perceive a dynamic, an attitude, that I find uncomfortable: that there is some spiritual authority outside the experience of these people, and that this authority, if tapped, will benefit the people as they live into the particularity of their collaborative experience. Conversations about spiritual experience should with far greater regularity move in the opposite direction. For example, a survivor of intimate partner violence, by virtue of his/her/hir experience and survival, has learned something—maybe many things—about God, about his/her/hir own soul. A survivor of trauma has things to teach hir faith community, things about religious tradition, theology, from which the church/theologians will benefit—things that will render a more authentic understanding of religious tradition and community, not just for that person and people who share that person's particular experience (of violence or trauma, for instance), but also and very importantly for everyone who is a follower of that faith tradition, a member of its global community. I want to encourage people who claim the mantle of Christianity to hone our ability to receive and embrace such perspectives as essential to the vivification of our tradition.

Why should nonqueer Christians care about this?

You may have noticed that in terms of my own identity, so far I have talked more about being a priest than about being a Christian. Christianity is the essential lens into my personal faith. The story of God's transgressive movement into human history is, for me, communicated most clearly in the Hebrew and Greek scriptures of the Judeo-Christian canon.[3] I am mesmerized by the God of Genesis, whose voice creates all we know and all we are; the God of the Exodus, murderous and liberating. I join the Hebrew prophets in responding to God's transfixing call, "*Hineni!* Here I am." I am brought to spiritual health—literally, "saved"—by my self-immersion in the dynamic events of Jesus's teaching, execution, and resurrection. I duke it out with Paul, trying to wrap my mind and heart around what he gets so right and what he gets so wrong in his heroic effort to break open conventional thinking and build a living, global church. Christian liturgy, the living of these stories, the worship of this God—there are few moments when I feel so alive as when I am engaged in that vital space, pulsing with God's presence. It is up there with really good sex, with fierce anger, with floating effortlessly on the ocean, with being overcome by the surf and pounded mercilessly onto abrasive sand.

There's no denying that I am a Christian, and I have no wish to deny it. I wish fervently that I could count my Christian identity on the same plane as my priesthood, as my queerness. But it is not a term I employ often when I am presenting myself to others. It would not make it into my "elevator moment" if I had to sell myself in under a minute to an as-yet-unengaged stranger. If you were to ask me why, I bet you would not be surprised by the answer. The word "Christian" itself has become a weapon of violence perpetrated on my queer siblings. And even though I utterly reject the homophobic, transphobic theologies and hermeneutics so readily embraced by too many Christians—reject them as an affront to Christianity itself—I cannot deny that they have tainted, even for me, the very name of our tradition. Of my tradition.

This is a problem. It is a problem for me, obviously, as it makes it difficult to explain myself to others and also complicates my profession of a faith that is vibrant within me. It is a problem for me as I have waded through the subtle and overt homophobia still at work within the Episcopal Church.

The problem is much bigger and far more troubling that the personal and personnel issues at work for one woman. Queer people have for a very long time been under assault, and the violence waged against us is almost always attributed to religious belief. Christianity is not the only world religion that has been twisted to justify hateful attack on queer people; however, the most vocal antigay activists in the United States are quick to identify themselves, nominally, as Christian.[4] And their antigay rhetoric, clothed in allegedly "Christian" teaching, has been exported in the guise of Christian evangelism to inform and energize movements to persecute queer people the world over.

It is increasingly clear that this is also a problem for mainline Christianity. The face of the Christian church has become, for many people and especially for many young adults, the face of intolerance. If you have engaged in conversation with many young adults in recent years and asked them about their spiritual leanings, I bet cash money you have heard something like this: "I have a sense that there is some kind of spirit out there, God maybe, and I care about it; but church? No, that's not for me."

This discomfort with Christianity is not confined to young adults in America. Even people in the church are affected by it. Come back with me to that elevator we were in a moment ago. It is likely that if you and I were to meet for the first time, very early on in our conversation—perhaps even in my elevator moment of introduction—I would disclose in some way that I am gay. Not all queer people do, but I pretty much wear it on my sleeve. Now, if you are queer, too, you might take that opportunity to tell me so. And we would both get that fabulous little charge that queer people get recognizing and being recognized by each other, that small but significant feeling of the home that we become for each other just by being ourselves together.

This sense of home is a feeling that Christians have known during times when followers of Jesus have been persecuted. The fish symbol was used to identify Christians to each other in the early days of the Roman Empire in much the same way that the lambda became a discreet symbol for queers in the mid-twentieth century. Corrie ten Boom was a Christian in the Dutch underground during World War II whose family was imprisoned for helping Jews escape the Holocaust. Her book *The Hiding Place* tells the story of her struggle to survive the concentration camp. In the film adaptation, there is a scene in which a fellow prisoner subtly displays a cross to "come out" to her as a Christian. It brings her no small comfort simply to know she is near someone who shares what is for her an essential identity marker, what is for her a kind of home.

Today, that sense of Christianity as home, as identity marker, seems mostly to be embraced by evangelical Christians; and I understand why. I know from my Arkansas childhood that for many people evangelicalism is rooted not in a desire to be part of a conservative political movement, but in a fierce need to feel the love of a God who sustains you as you go about living what may be a very, very hard life. This is especially true for poor people, and especially in rural areas as predominate in the South.

I know that if I were to come out as Christian, there is a good chance that whomever I was introducing myself to would assume that I meant I was an evangelical Christian. Let's say I'm introducing myself to you. If you are queer, the assumption that I am an evangelical Christian might put you off. It might even strike fear in your heart. That is exactly the opposite of what I want to have happen when I meet another queer person. That likelihood alone makes it very difficult for me to feel good about identifying myself as a Christian when I first meet someone.

Let's say you identify as straight, but you regularly attend a progressive church. How likely are you to meet my introduction with an enthusiastic, "Oh, I'm a Christian, too!"? If you are like most of the people I hang out with in progressive churches, you might hold off on that disclosure because you don't want to run the risk of me assuming that *you* are an evangelical. Or, if you are assuming that I am an evangelical, maybe you don't want to bond with me. Evangelical and progressive Christians really are just not the same animal, and you may feel that our views of our faith are so different that there is no real bond to explore. Or worse, you might assume that we will be antagonistic toward each other, which might be anathema to your sense of Christian identity. So, does outing yourself as Christian give you a spark of hope for that little feel-good moment of home? Not likely.

This is a huge problem for those of us on the Christian Left. The question of how we witness to our faith is vexing for mainline Christians, and over the past four decades we have gotten almost no traction in figuring it out. During that span of time, the evangelical Right has become more and more visible, claiming exclusive right to the title of "Christian" with greater and greater audacity.

Who are we? What do we believe? How do we tell other people about it?

A church that cannot answer these questions will not survive. It will certainly never be a force that effects change broadly. It will never be the force that progressive Christianity is meant to be, witnessing to the transgressive, invasive, earth-altering power of divine love that this world so desperately needs.

This is an important issue to me, as a priest and as a Christian who is dog tired of having the lens of her faith distorted, misunderstood, and turned into a weapon. But it is only part of my purpose in writing. In recent years, mainline Christianity has made important strides in shifting the terms of religious conversation about sexuality from the *issue* of homosexuality to the value inherent in the *people* whose lives are involved in this conversation. Within those lives—our lives—is a pattern of experience, an ethical trajectory that places extraordinary spiritual demands on the individuals in its path. Queer individuals are called to perceive a truth inside themselves, name it as an identity marker, reckon with it, tell the truth about it even in the face of hostility, find others who perceive a comparable identity marker, and build community for the betterment of all of us. That, to me, is the essence of a spiritual journey. It is more than that. In my faith tradition, we refer to this as a call. It is a vocation.

I want to invite Christians to observe queer virtue and learn from it. We live in a time when people looking for moral example may look everywhere *except* to the church for it. The church's moral authority has been badly compromised in recent years by highly visible moral lapses as well as by an obdurate determination by some of our most visible denominations to cling to regressive and oppressive theologies and practices—hostile to women,

LGBTQ people, non-Christians, urban dwellers, and the list could go on and on—increasingly rejected by common sense and basic human compassion. In denominations that are more progressive, such as the Episcopal Church, too often the church seems to be following the moral leadership of others, including the secular LGBTQ movement, rather than leading. I know that this is one of the reasons my Christian ethical compass is less robust than my queer ethical compass: the LGBTQ community has been providing bold moral leadership for decades. The church can learn from this, must learn from this example. Within progressive Christianity there are countless people and communities who are living quietly but faithfully the teachings of Jesus, who are witnessing to the ethical mandates of our Judeo-Christian heritage. Given the power and integrity of this witness, the progressive church can and should square its shoulders and provide moral authority to people who hunger for it. One important way to do this is to acknowledge the moral witness of other communities, to celebrate them, honor them, and learn from them.

It is not hard to perceive how this might work and why it matters. Consider, for example, Martin Luther King Jr.'s appeal to white clergy in his "Letter from a Birmingham Jail." Consider the risk that those white clerics faced as they pondered his appeal. Now consider the quality of Christian witness that King was calling on them to display and proclaim by listening to his words. Decades later, the letter still inspires and challenges people of faith to comprehend the justice that God demands, and to dig into our own souls, try to show the courage that Dr. King was showing, and take even a fraction of the risk that he and so many others were taking in pursuit of justice, of dignity.

"Lift Every Voice and Sing" now appears in the Episcopal Hymnal. It is a hymn that has resonance for anyone who has known oppression, and yet its roots as the "Negro National Anthem" are what give it both its meaning and its power. Who can sing this hymn and not remember the story that Maya Angelou tells in *I Know Why the Caged Bird Sings* of the devastating, determined spiritual journey she made on the day of her eighth grade graduation?[5] And is there not something of this devastation and determination that informed the decisions of churches across the United

States to post signs outside their walls in 2014 and 2015 declaring to the world that "Black Lives Matter"? We are not even close to where we need to be in addressing racism in our faith communities, let alone in our world. But for those of all races within the church who do indeed take black lives seriously, the witness of this movement has powerfully shaped our understanding of what Christian faith is, and what it calls us to be and to do.

In lifting up the moral witness of queer life, I wish for two outcomes: First, that progressive Christians will rise up to demand a full stop on the frontal assault being waged on queer people in the name of religion. Not just because such assault is blasphemous to any understanding of the Christian impulse, but also and importantly because to deny the inherent worth of queer people is simply a lie. Second, that progressive Christianity will look to queerness as a lens for vivifying our expressions of faith, both personal and corporate, theological and liturgical. To the extent that progressive Christians see the potential value of such exploration, I want to encourage it.

During Holy Week in 2008, I attended a remarkable presentation on the Triduum—the three days that stretch from Maundy Thursday to Easter Sunday. The presentation was given by the Right Reverend Jeffrey D. Lee, bishop of Chicago, a man whose primary impulse is to breathe life into our understanding and experience of worship. He spoke about the ancient traditions at work in the liturgies of those three days, the meaning they held for the ancient church, and the remnants we bring into our services today. Toward the end of his presentation, he asked us to gaze upon an icon of Christ stepping back through the door of the tomb, back into the world of the living. The bishop talked about Jesus, in that moment, rupturing everything that human beings understand about life and death. I was mesmerized, moved to tears by the power of his witness.

Later that day, I returned to my office at the Episcopal campus ministry at Northwestern University. I saw several students, and told them about the bishop's presentation, about his use of the word "rupture" to describe what Jesus had done. Now, you have to understand, for anyone who has spent any time studying queer theory, the word "rupture" is iconic, a code word that evocatively captures the essence of the movement. The word was not lost on my students. "Really? 'Ruptured'? He said 'ruptured'?" When I assured them that this was the word he had used, it appeared that the bishop, and Jesus, had risen in their esteem.

This story goes a long way toward illustrating how I think an appreciation for queerness can benefit progressive Christianity. Not only is queerness true to what Christianity is about, it also takes people by surprise. It is alive, and exciting. It communicates the power of the Christian gospel in ways that thoughtful, intrepid seekers can hear.

Having expressed that sentiment, it is important to be very clear about what this book is not. This is not an attempt to tell queer people that they "should be" anything other than the extraordinary souls they already are. This is not an attempt to define the spiritual life of any queer person without hir consent, in any way, or even to impose the notion of spirituality on queer people who have rejected that notion for themselves. Queer atheists have nothing to fear from me. I intend only the deepest respect for my LGBTQ sisters and brothers and genderqueer siblings, and for the choices and definitions they apply to their interior lives.

A powerful motivation for me in writing is the fervent desire to spread balm on the vast wounds of my people, to tend to the immense damage done to queer people and queer souls in the name of religion. My perspective is a spiritual one, and I see my queer tribe through a spiritual lens. What I see are experiences, truths, journeys, and ethics that, for me, have deep spiritual meaning. This book is certainly an attempt to point to that meaning *as I see it*, and as I believe anyone who embraces a spiritual worldview—and explicitly, a Christian worldview—should see it as well.

Thus there is a persistent subtext here, which is a love song to my people. If in hearing that love song a queer person is moved to view himself with deeper love, to perceive herself as a person of greater value, that is all to the good. Also, importantly, if such ones find themselves feeling God's extraordinary touch, or *naga*, or hear God's encouraging voice whispering into their ear—"You go, girl"; "You go, boy"; "You go, you fabulous genderqueer child"—well, *awesome*.

This project explores several aspects of queer experience that inform queer identity. In part 1, I will discuss the nuances of queer virtue, paying specific attention to resonance with vital teachings in Christian tradition. I hope to lend theological heft to a populist call for a moratorium on religious-based violence against queer people, recognizing such violence to be not just offensive but blasphemous. In part 2, I will discuss how specific aspects of the lived experience of queer people might help invigorate contemporary Christian practice. Taken together, it is my hope that this work will provide trajectories for Christian inquiry that could bring new energy and urgency to the progressive church and its proclamation of the gospel. If the prospect of such inquiry stirs up a little burst of excitement, of joy in the hearts of my nonqueer Christian siblings, again I say, *awesome*.

PART I

THE PATH OF QUEER VIRTUE

CHAPTER 1

ON THE INHERENT QUEERNESS
OF CHRISTIANITY

A faint light glows in the eastern sky.
In the garden, it is still dark, shapes just beginning
to form hazily before her eyes.
A woman has come to weep.

Wait, is this a garden? No, it is a cemetery. As the light slowly grows—lavender, to rose, to peach—the tombs slowly become visible—black to grey. Where is the one she seeks? The stone, freshly laid, should stand out, whiter than the tomb. Wait, where is it? This is the right place, isn't it? Still so dark, the dew making everything damp, softening every line. Everything about this place is disorienting. It is so still, so quiet. She can almost believe the events of the past few days are just a bad, bad dream. But no, this is it. This is the one.

What greets this woman is not a white stone, but a black, empty cave. Something is very wrong here. His body is gone. Her stomach lurches. Please, no, this can't be right. After all we've been through, is it really not over? Can't we just be done, grieve, begin to move on without him?

This place, this half-lit, predawn place, garden and cemetery, mistily rising from night to day, from life to death and back again to life: this is the place, the crucial cosmic moment that will launch a new faith tradition, a new way of perceiving the essence and the promise of God.

It is not happenstance that this moment is so fully, so exquisitely shot through with liminality. The woman is Mary Magdalene, a figure perpetually described as living on the margin of her society. As such, she is uniquely situated to perceive this moment. Every one of her senses would have been alive with the sounds, sights, smells, touch of this particular time on this particular morning. If you've ever been awake in that hazy quiet—so quiet—that in-between place when so much of the world has yet to wake up, you know: there is nothing quite like the depth of transition that is taking place here, now. It surrounds you, envelops you.

And yet it is changing. Even if you want to stay in that moment, you can't linger. Things move here, sensual experience shifts. Something new is happening, and you know it, feel it, breathe it in with every passing minute.

It is not an accident that humanity, embodied in this woman, first encounters the resurrection here, in this place, at this time. Mary has entered a threshold, one that communicates perfectly the nature of a God who will not be contained, whose dynamic, fierce love cannot be killed and cannot be tamed. What is happening here is very queer indeed; and while the fissure is most visible here and now, what is queer about it is not confined to this single liminal moment.

Christianity makes three truth claims that distinguish it from any other faith tradition:

That God came to earth in the person of Jesus Christ.

That Jesus Christ was killed, died, and rose from the dead.

That it is possible for any human being to perceive these truths and to join or form a community that worships this God, following the ethical path laid out by Jesus.

These three truth claims form the backbone of Christian faith. Each one dramatically and decisively ruptures a binary that previously was thought to be inviolable:

That God and humanity are fundamentally distinct from each other. Before Jesus, many traditions posited the idea that gods could pose as mortals; Judaism had asserted that human beings were made in God's image, an emanation and reflection of the divine. The Sumerian and Greek pantheons included demigods who were half human and half god, but whose partial humanity impeded full exercise of their divine power. Christianity asserted something much different. Grappling with the question of who Jesus was and how he was composed, early church leaders declared that Jesus was "fully God and fully human."[1]

That life and death stand in opposition to each other. On one level, this binary is an iteration of the one above, marking the distinction between God and humanity. God, by definition, is immortal: always and permanently alive. Humans are mortal: in terms of our corporeal existence, death always wins in the end. Christianity asserts that Jesus, fully divine and fully human, really truly died, and really truly came back to life. Jesus thus not only ruptures the ideas that God cannot die and that humans cannot return from death, but something more: Jesus effects all of this by traveling through death itself. Resurrection insists that experiences of death are an essential component of a life truly lived. Life and death are thus not eternally separate, but coexist in dynamic tension, interacting, constantly informing each other. This is the essence of Christian liberation, the salvation wrought by Jesus's life, death, and resurrection: God does not hesitate to enter into our experiences of death, to travel through death with us. And the upshot is profound. Christianity boldly proclaims that for human beings, death is never the last word.

That religious belief and practice are part and parcel of tribal, ethnic, or national identity, staking out boundaries that are crossed at the expense of family bonds, social cohesion, and moral rectitude. Christianity transgresses these kinds of bonds, asserting that every human heart has the ability to perceive God in the person of Jesus Christ and to comprehend the salvific liberation effected by Jesus's resurrection. And yet Christianity is not a solitary path; it is deeply, intentionally relational, designed to be lived out in community. Thus Christianity persistently calls people whose hearts perceive its truths to create or join communities of faith, communities that may dovetail with ethnic

or national identities but that can include a remarkably
diverse array of members; communities that live into an
ethic based on the teachings of Jesus, proclaiming Christ's
role in breaking open the cosmic forces described above.

This is why authentic Christianity is and must be queer. We
stand in that garden, our feet damp with the dew, looking up into
a lavender pink sky about to explode into gold, marveling at the
irrepressible life force that surrounds us, calls to us, demands our
attention. Christianity is an invitation into movement, into change.
It may contain moments of stunning simplicity, but it is never
simplistic. It is designed to challenge simplistic efforts to grasp, to
contain, and to tame both God and our experience of God. Christianity is a path that incessantly leads you to places you've never
been before. Like the parables that were the hallmark of Jesus's
teaching, if this path doesn't surprise you, it isn't doing its job.

WHY DOES IT MATTER TO RUPTURE BINARIES?
WHY WOULD GOD CARE ABOUT THAT?

One of the most challenging aspects of human existence is perceiving and negotiating a healthy relationship between Self and Other.
Our lives are a complex mix of deep connection to one another and
to God on the one hand, and experiences of profound isolation
on the other. We exist in bodies that constantly remind us both of
the ways that we are connected to each other and of the ways we
are separate from others, different from others. Our bodies are
capable of interacting powerfully with other bodies, bringing us
closer to ecstasy, to the sacred. They can also sustain damage, and
do damage.

That mix of interconnection and isolation exists not just at an
individual level. Our corporeal selves also join with others to form
corporate entities. We exist within communities that are intercon-
nected with other communities and that can be isolated from other
communities. Our need of one another is fierce. Our ability to
harm one another is vast.

It is impossible to comprehend God's experience of this apparent dichotomy. God, not confined to a physical form, may not
experience such intense complexity regarding Self and Other. Per-

haps this is part of what it means to be created in God's image: we have the ability to perceive spiritual connection to Others that is not bound by the limits of our skin, or the borders of our lands.

What we know for sure is that this business of negotiating Self and Other is a mixed bag, often fraught, and occasionally exhilarating. We know that there is tension between the states of being connected and isolated. And somehow, it is our identity as creatures of God that constantly demands that these two states of being interact, inform each other. Which is to say, it is our identity as creatures of God, made in the image of God, that constantly ruptures whatever impulse we may have to cast our connection and isolation as binary states, existing on opposite ends of a continuum from each other.

This is a dynamic in which each of us is immersed every day of our lives. It is the tension we navigate as individuals who need the love of our families but who sometimes go a little crazy trying to share the same bathroom. It is the tension that confronts us when our nations or tribes are trying to build productive relationships with each other, but find ourselves descending into armed conflict. It is the tension that tears into you when the person you love desperately has just broken your heart.

Living into that tension in a healthy way can be very hard. How do you understand yourself and your individuality in a way that comprehends what connects you to others? How do you understand the ways that you are different from others, separate from others, while comprehending the vital importance of our diversity? What happens when our needs compete? What happens when resources are scarce? What happens when someone gets hurt?

Philosophers and theologians from Lao Tzu to Abraham Joshua Heschel have pondered these questions throughout human history. A healthy approach to Self and Other is a balancing act, and the impulse to create binaries—and especially false binaries—can throw a person or a community off balance. Consciously inverting those binaries makes it possible to get one's balance back. But again we must ask the question: Why would God care one way or the other about this?

God may have set up this business of figuring out Self and Other as an essential part of the human journey. The negotiation of Self and Other so pervades both our existential concerns and our daily life that I have a hard time imagining that God didn't intend us to wrestle with it consciously. But God's intention aside, there is no question that our ability to navigate the relationship between Self and Other profoundly affects the quality of our lives, in ways that most certainly matter to God. When we navigate it well, we build each other up. When we get it wrong, we damage ourselves and one another.

Sometimes the damage is extreme. One way people get it wrong is by radicalizing the separation of Self and Other. Perhaps the worst version of this happens when the Other becomes cast not just as different, but as despised. Now, I'm not talking about the phenomenon of not liking someone else; nor am I talking about the anger and even rage you may feel toward someone who has hurt you. The Despised Other is someone who has become so alien to you that you stop being able to conceive of that person as human. That person may become simply a screen upon which you project your worst pain and fear. This is a place of profound danger, spiritually. It can certainly be dangerous for the person who has been dehumanized; an enormous amount of violence, including genocide, is justified in this way. But it is also dangerous for the person who despises the Other. Here is where some of our worst sins are committed.

The inverse of the Despised Other would be the collapse of those categories as distinct at all. Co-opting the Other into one's Self can be a profoundly abusive act. Sometimes the collapse is the result of a kind of suffocating faux love. Sometimes it is born of privilege that simply fails to perceive that there are others present who are markedly different. It can happen in churches, both in local congregations and in sweeping gestures of global reach. Either way, as with the invention of the Despised Other, the end result is an erasure of the Other's humanity, rendering a person or community invisible or nonexistent.

These are extreme situations, to be sure, but the fundamental balancing act in navigating the relationship between Self and Other exists for all of us. You and I could come up with hundreds of daily, mundane situations in which clarity about Self and Other is something that you have to figure out, with outcomes that affect your well-being or the well-being of another person. Understanding and negotiating one's sense of self and one's connection to others, drawing appropriate boundaries while maintaining necessary interconnection, is of vital importance. Getting it right may be the core ethical challenge of the human condition.

Christianity worships a God who disrupts any glib or easy notion of what Self and Other are, constantly challenging us to hit a "reset" button in our efforts to comprehend how we are supposed to relate to ourselves, to one another, and to this God.

Throughout history, human beings have employed binaries as a way of conceiving the relationship between Self and Other. Sometimes binaries are created to help one make sense of oneself, to ease intestinal uncertainty or discomfort about one's identity or inherent value. There is a certain comfort in knowing who I am at a very basic level. There is a certain comfort, to me, in knowing who you are at a basic level. The desire to comprehend oneself is a good thing; however, the urge to create binaries as a tool for such comprehension can be deeply problematic, especially when those binaries are overly rigid or simply false. Sometimes binaries are imposed on others not in an attempt to make meaning but in order to achieve self-serving ends. Sometimes in matters political or religious, binaries are established with the specific intention to set Those People apart from Us.

False binaries can create painful spiritual quandaries. As a priest, I have spent a great deal of time counseling people who are consumed with the basic question, "Does this thing I've done/this feeling I have make me a bad person?" As if good and bad were mutually exclusive. As if one slip can leave a person permanently stained.

Binaries are often fraught with moral complexity, and moral danger. That's why they are such an important matter as one discerns and negotiates the relationship between Self and Other, and it's why any religious tradition worth its salt takes them very seriously. Christianity—authentic Christianity—incessantly dukes it out with binaries, constantly questioning them and rejecting them when they get out of hand or prove wrong. It makes perfect sense that Christianity would do this. Christianity focuses intently on our relationships with one another, encouraging and demanding essential health in our interactions and interconnections.

Let's go back to that garden, that cemetery. Imagine yourself in that light, waiting for the sun to rise. You have to open your eyes as wide as they can go in order to see anything. You have to allow forms to come into shape so that you can make sense of them. All of your senses are alive, awake. This is a place where you have to be ready for anything. Maybe you are simply allowing yourself to perceive all that is coming at you, quietly, peacefully. Maybe you are hungry to make meaning of it, to move forward with purpose and clarity. Maybe you are standing stock still, amazed to be surrounded by so much mystery, so much beauty, so much that is so different from what surrounds you during the routine, glaring, familiar light of midday.

The God I worship is One who shows up in moments like this, constantly taking me by surprise, constantly showing me things that I only barely perceived before. I have come to believe that this is an essential quality of God's love for us, this ability to surprise and amaze us, and that it is one of the most extraordinary gifts that God gives us. I have come to believe that it is built into whatever purpose God had in creating us in the first place.

This means that God's revelations to us are very often doing at least two vitally important things. First, they are shaking up our attachments to binaries in which we are getting something wrong, messing up our ability to live well. Second, they are imploring us to perceive with wonder realities that are almost too amazing, too sublime, to grasp. To walk the Christian path is to encounter God's self-revelation, which constantly advances both of these ends—shaking us up, and breaking us open. Both of these ends have something to do with liberating us, which is to say: God queers our world, our lives, our hearts in order to set us free.

WHAT DOES IT MEAN TO SAY THAT CHRISTIANITY IS A PATH?

Before the term "Christian" was coined, followers of Jesus knew themselves to be involved in the tradition of Judaism, even as they were articulating and forming new beliefs and practices. Trying to name what distinguished their movement, they described themselves as being part of the *hodos*, a Greek word translated in the Acts of the Apostles as "the way." The word literally refers to a road, or the journey that one makes on a road.

It is a path that one journeys with others. Christian ethics are deeply informed by the sensibility, inherited from Judaism, that our community is a kind of family. According to Jesus, the dominant characteristic of this community is supposed to be love: "By this everyone will know that you are my disciples, if you have love for one another."[2] Paul clarified that this love is no gooey emotion, but is rather a commitment to one another, a hard-won discipline that demands the best in oneself and looks for the best in others: that "bears all things, believes all things, hopes all things."[3] For Paul, love was the glue that holds a community together. But that love was never designed to be insular. Rather, the evangelistic impulse is precisely about expanding that sense of love outward both in proclamation and in service to the larger community. This was one of the significant ways that Christianity diverged from Judaism, becoming a community that transgresses ethnic ties, hoping to expand in scope and scale to include those in need throughout the entire world.

Historically, this notion of Christianity as a path has been visible in many forms. We can see it among those who embrace contemplative life, often as members of religious orders. It is plainly visible in our sacramental traditions, in which the sacred is invoked to mark and sanctify life events such as birth, marriage, death; in daily rituals of prayer; and weekly gatherings to celebrate the mass, also known as the Eucharistic feast. Among those Protestant denominations for whom sacrament is less central, the path has long been manifest as a relationship to scripture and an effort to bring scriptural teachings to bear in one's daily life.

It has always been true that different kinds of Christians tend to gravitate toward different aspects of the three essential Christian proclamations I spelled out earlier. Thus today some Christians strongly emphasize faith in the first two, which might be called the "cosmic events" of Jesus's incarnation and resurrection. Faith in these events is crucial to what evangelicals see as faith in Jesus as a personal Lord and Savior. Other Christians place less emphasis on the cosmic aspects of Jesus's mission, preferring to focus more on his teachings as the basis for ethical life. Oftentimes progressive

Christian communities are far more interested in how people treat one another—expressed in commitments to justice and inclusion—than in cosmic truth claims about Jesus's Lordship.

These movements, which involve millions of people who have myriad and complex attachments to diverse aspects of the Christian tradition, cannot be oversimplified. Authentic participation in Christianity will encounter all three of these truth claims and must deal with each of them. Leaning too far in any one direction creates a significant barrier to authentic proclamation of the Christian gospel. When some Christians treat the cosmic claims about Christ as a litmus test determining whether you are justified in the eyes of God, many people are repelled—and harmed—and the evangelistic enterprise is thwarted. When other Christians dismiss the cosmic claims as unimportant or irrelevant to the path, the entire enterprise becomes theologically unmoored. These dynamics all by themselves go a long way toward explaining the challenge that Christians across the spectrum face in speaking as credible moral voices in today's world.

Many queer people have been burned by Christian proclamation that leans too far toward rigid moralism. Many people of faith have grown weary of tepid Christian proclamations that, in the name of inclusion, fail to hold anyone to account. One side is soul crushing; the other is boring. How do we find our way back to the electric predawn, earth-altering moment in that garden?

What always guides me back is an appreciation for the inherent liminality of the tradition. I never cease to wonder at the frequency with which my queer identity and experience pop into view as I am studying scripture, pondering a sermon, or engaging someone in a pastoral conversation. I have long had to restrain the impulse to bring queer insight to bear explicitly. If I did so every time it occurs to me, that's almost all I'd talk about.

Attention to the queerness of our tradition has the potential to shed light on the part that progressives tend not to proclaim well: the content, the theological heft. Queerness can do this with particular potency for two reasons: First, because queer identity is itself the topic of some of the most energetic conversation between theology and ethics today, both within faith traditions and in secular society. Second, because LGBTQ people already speak the ethical language that is so familiar to this wing of the faith tradition. Which is to say, queerness can also be understood as a kind of path.

As with the Christian path, walking the path of queerness with honesty and some measure of integrity makes possible a kind of virtue. The path of queer virtue looks something like this:

One discerns an identity;

One risks telling oneself and others about that identity;

One engages with others, touches others, to explore that identity;

One confronts and is confronted by scandal;

One lives out one's identity with and through community, looking to the margins to see who is not yet included.

Queer experience cannot be systematized. There is something about the image of a path that illuminates the relationship between these various experiences that LGBTQ people encounter, but that image is defiantly not rigid; there is nothing "step-by-step" about it. In fact, it is the nature of queerness to resist being neatly ordered. That resistance to ordering is one of the particular gifts of my people, and it is also one of the qualities that most puts us in touch with the divine (which, you may have noticed, also resists order). So don't even begin to imagine a neat, well-trimmed walkway. If queerness is indeed a path, it is wild and chaotic, overgrown, twisting and turning back on itself, at times plunging into deep pools of unknown liquid, then emerging suddenly onto dry ground. On this path, the future is often so murky that you can't see your hand in front of your face. Then suddenly you turn a corner, and a breathtaking vista opens before you.

Nothing on this path is once and done. The demands of this path—the obstacles and opportunities—interact with one another. They may take place in any order, and are likely to be repeated, exacting more precise demands all the time. A queer person lives them over and over again. None of us walks the path perfectly, and some queer folk are not able or flat out refuse to walk parts of it at all. But it constantly amazes me how dedicated my community is to this path, on the whole, and how hard we work both to stay on it and to make it accessible, possible, for others.

To the extent that queer experience can be conceived as a path, it bears a remarkable resemblance to the path of Christian virtue. And this is also clear: what I know about Christian virtue, about Christianity as a path, I have learned primarily from walking this queer path every day of my life.

I am one of those progressive Christians who for years evaded a direct encounter with the cosmic truth claims of Christianity. But in grappling with the queerness of my tradition, I have begun to understand with depth and clarity the import of the astonishing theological claims made by Christianity. It is possible to gaze upon the incarnation, the Christ event, and the resurrection not as rigid, take-it-or-leave-it doctrines, but as true sources of liberation and hope. It is possible to talk about them passionately, without threatening psychic or spiritual harm to other queer people, or women, or children, or anyone else who knows what it is to be the target of religious bullying. Queerness can be a powerful lens, helping Christians proclaim our faith with pride, in a way that issues a genuine invitation to others to participate in something we know to be truly life giving. Queerness has, perhaps ironically, helped me understand what honest evangelism—life-giving evangelism—can look and sound like. For all of these reasons, I am come to believe that progressive Christianity would benefit simply by being more intentional about allowing queer voices to speak freely, particularly in leadership positions, and by listening carefully to these voices.

Why should we do this?

First, Christianity is inherently liminal, inherently queer. Many queer people possess a visceral understanding of these dynamics. We are uniquely positioned to ponder, perceive, and make visible what is most alive, vexing, and fabulous about this aspect of the Christian tradition.

Second, there is tremendous resonance between the paths of Queer and Christian virtue.

Third, many queer people are deeply motivated to do this work. This interest is personal because it involves claiming our lives and proclaiming our integrity. It is political, because it is a way to push back against forces that continue to oppress us.

And for vast numbers of us, it is deeply spiritual. Christianity has always been most vibrant and most prophetic at times and in places where people are struggling to overcome injustice. In today's world, LGBTQ people know as much as anyone about what it means to hunger for spiritual connection and to have roadblock after roadblock thrown up by the people who most visibly keep the official gates.

This book is an attempt to breathe fresh air into public conversations about both queerness and the Christian tradition. The chapters that follow explore aspects of what I am calling the path of queer virtue, as enumerated above. Each chapter reflects on what it is like to encounter these aspects of queer experience and spells out where and how Christians encounter these same issues, explaining how an appreciation for queerness might help Christians better understand and better navigate the path.

CHAPTER 2

IDENTITY

Hello. I'm Johnny Cash.

That deep masculine voice, oozing raw confidence and bare pain, exists in my earliest catalog of memory. It was how he introduced himself, his music, his gritty take on love and the world. I must have been about five years old when I first registered his voice on the stereo, on television. Johnny Cash always introduced himself before he performed. Even as a small child I think I identified with him. I understood the significance of being able to say, "This is who I am. Let me tell you what I know."

KINDERGARTEN

This was the year I came to consciousness of the world around me. My family was living outside of St. Louis. I remember sitting on the living room floor watching Walter Cronkite's news broadcasts with my dad. War was stirring in Southeast Asia. I remember news footage of soldiers in jungle-like settings very different from the landscape I knew. Martin Luther King Jr.'s assassination is the first world event I remember.

I was also coming to consciousness of myself. My kindergarten had an informal dress code—not enforced, just understood by all of us. Girls were supposed to wear dresses. I didn't really think much about it. Then one day, a girl in my class arrived wearing pants. She commanded my full attention. I was surprised, and vaguely scandalized. But mostly, I was amazed at her courage. How could she choose to stand out like that? Why wasn't she dressed like the rest of us? And come to think of it, why did we always wear dresses to school, anyway?

Dresses were not my attire of choice outside of school. I was a tomboy who instantly recognized Scout in *To Kill a Mockingbird* as a soul mate. One day, my mother took me shopping for shoes. I wanted sneakers, and to get them at that time, I had to wander into the boys' section of the store. I found an awesome pair, and presented them to the clerk. Dismayed, he turned to my mother and said, "Those are boys' shoes." "Yes," said my mother, cutting off further discussion. "Size four, please."

It is not a surprise to me that so many memories, the clearest of my early childhood, center on gender identity. It was a big issue for me, a dominant thread in the fabric of my self-awareness that helped me make sense of my life when I came out as a lesbian. I am not alone in this. Coming-out stories for people my age are often punctuated by the refrain, "I look back on my life now, and it all makes sense. At some level, I've always known." When I came out, my dad apparently struggled a bit. Had something happened to me? he wondered. Had he done something wrong? My stepmother gently corrected him, "Norman, this is Liz. Think back. This has always been in her, her whole life."

I've heard so many LGBTQ people look back on their childhoods and say, "I was always just . . . different." Difference can become the window for perception of self, and sometimes, it is the difference itself that becomes the identity marker. What I mean is, it is possible for marginalized people to become aware of ourselves as "Other" in Simone de Beauvoir's sense,[1] and to perceive that otherness as the driver that marks us, that is at work in us. Much of the work for queer justice—for any justice movement—involves transcending this fixation on otherness. Proclaiming our inherent value requires that we recognize, name, and celebrate our identity as queer people. That is, shifting the focus from the external disapprobation of our otherness—and the political subjugation it breeds—to an interior knowledge of ourselves. It is in this shift that Pride emerges, that empowerment is made possible.

In this regard, I was lucky. My entire family, both sides, for generations, has been made up of people who bucked the tide. My father's family were Swedish immigrants who left all they knew to travel to America in the late nineteenth century. My Edman grandparents were missionaries to Ecuador before they settled in Wheaton, Illinois, where my grandfather eventually took the helm of Wheaton College. My mother's people were journalists and preachers, pioneers who left their homes to travel west to Arkansas and Tennessee. My great-aunt, Elizabeth Burrow, ran our family newspaper in 1957 during the desegregation of the Arkansas public schools. She was one of three editors in the state who had the guts to oppose Orval Faubus in his efforts to keep black students out of Little Rock Central High. And that was just one aspect of her nonconformity. She also had converted to Catholicism at a young age, its own scandal in the Protestant town of Ozark, Arkansas. She never married, and counted Dorothy Day among her close friends.

Aunt Elizabeth stands out for me because of her prophetic voice; but she was not the only member of that family to hold strong and controversial opinions, many of which I do not wear with pride. My point here is merely to say that I grew up in a family in which people spoke the truth as they saw it. Members of my family were individuals, fiercely so, with their own opinions, quirks, gracious and difficult, quarrelsome and kind. I come from an eccentric bunch. Which is to say, being "different" was already part of my DNA. The challenge and the gift in this was that, from a very early age, I had to find my own identity—not just "different," but "me." And from my earliest days, that identity was manifest as something bound up in my gender and sexuality.

There is another memory from my five-year-old experience that is big for me. My best friend lived next door. We were nearly inseparable. For some reason that I don't remember, my mother saw fit to put us into a bathtub together. Cleaning up after a mud fight? I have no idea. I think that at least one of us was in a bathing suit, but even that is not clear to me. The memory is an interior one, the strong and clear sense that this moment held something I desired—a degree of closeness to my best friend, closer than what we had experienced in our yards or at school, or even in our occasional sleepovers (me on the floor, her in her bed). She had had something like the sneaker buying experience, too, and we were comrades in our explicit chafing against the constraints of gender conformity. "I just wish I were a boy," she said to me one day as we stood in her driveway, waiting for the bus. My eyes widened with hope, surprise, a burst of something that connected us even more closely to each other. "Me, too! Me, too!"

This memory is important because it was my first movement toward someone who shared what was already emerging as an identity marker for me. And this movement, this sojourning, is itself characteristic of queer identity. Though my family may have been eccentric, I was not delivered into the arms of people who regularly wore gender-nonconforming clothing or were drawn like magnets to people of the same sex. To understand this part of myself, to nurture and feed it, I had to find others like me. The story about my best friend in kindergarten reveals something significant: I began looking for others, for community, at a very young age.[2]

Lisa Kron and Jeanine Tesori exquisitely capture a childhood moment of queer connection in *Fun Home*, their musical adaptation of Alison Bechdel's graphic memoir. In the showstopping number "Ring of Keys," small Alison encounters a butch delivery woman. Watching this woman, Alison is mesmerized for reasons she can't even name. Something in this woman's manner and attire illuminates Alison's interior world like a flare. Though they have never met and may never meet again, Alison knows that she is connected to this woman, that they are kindred in some important way.

The desire for connection to others may have been bound up for many of us in a desire for guidance about how to live. These stories point toward the early development of ethical impulses rooted in sexual identity. It is a story, an ethical process, that countless queer children have lived out for centuries, arguably for all of human history. What I am describing here, what I lived as a child, is simply a natural response, a lived response, to the fact of my queer identity.

I don't have any idea what it may have looked like in years past or in other cultures for queer children to discern their identity. Others need to fill in what this process may have looked like then, or what it looks like today, whether in the United States or in other locations, or what it looks like for children who find their identities on some other point on the LGBTQ spectrum. But in the United States, in the mid-twentieth century, in a privileged and powerful nation fixated on dualisms—good/evil, north/south, black/white, capitalist/communist, rich/poor, male/female—discerning a queer identity looked something like this:

First, there was an awareness of being different. Something in me did not fit into the binary conceptions of reality that surrounded me. My awareness was focused on the gender binary. I simply was not a girl in the same sense that most of the girls and women around me seemed to be. The dress code, the expected behaviors, the nervous giggles about coupling with men or boys that began at a shockingly young age, none of this felt right—not in the sense of right or wrong, but in the sense of personal fit.

At some point I realized that this difference was affecting my uptake of the world around me. Thankfully, I grew up in a time when American attachment to binaries in general was being openly questioned and challenged. The 1960s and '70s were indeed turbulent, a wrenching of the social order that we are still sorting out. My life has played out over the course of incredible disruption—and not just my life. Yours, too. This is the story of our times: social disruption, vast changes in economic reality, astounding advances in human communications technologies, the democratization of travel, an immensely heightened awareness of ourselves as global citizens, and in the midst of all this change, a search for connection and for meaning rooted in . . . something.

I began to look inside myself—prayerfully, I would say—for a sense of rootedness, for clarity about who I am and what my life is supposed to be about. The perception of an identity can and should become the ground not just for a rejection of ideas that don't ring true, but for the embrace of that which *is* true. This is something Johnny Cash taught me. Telling people who you are is the first step to singing your songs. It sets the stage for you to tell people, with courage, both the lies and the truths as you see them.

My search for meaning, for purpose, has always been rooted in my identity as a queer person. This was true even before I was consciously aware of it. I have always possessed an innate sense, for one thing, that simplistic binaries are seldom valid. I have always known that binaries tended to shut down conversation and human connection, and that part of my call was to open up lines of communication, to encourage a more nuanced view of human experience and transcendent reality.

Very little of this ethical discernment has been detached, or merely intellectual. My ethical development was/is a lived process, a relational process, in which I was/am coming to know myself even as I simultaneously learn how to meet my fierce need for human connection with others.

HIGH SCHOOL

I remember vividly that day in Trigonometry, as I sat at my desk working out a formula, my head cupped in my hand. In the next aisle, a seat behind me, my friend Cathy crossed her leg. It was spring; she was wearing a skirt. Such an ordinary movement for her, but it set me on fire. Through the crook in my arm, I saw the flesh of her calf muscle, her shin, as a wave of heat exploded from my groin to my head. My entire body flushed. It was the most extraordinary, fiercely pleasurable sensation I had ever felt. "What was *that*?" I wondered, almost aloud, amazed by the ecstatic charge still coursing through me.

And then, half a beat later: Cathy. Whatever had just happened was a reaction to a girl. "What *was* that?!" In that moment I knew that whatever had just happened was not just about Cathy, it was also about me. Something about me was different from what I had up til that moment expected myself to be. And yet, I also knew in a flash that it was not alien. It was not different from who I was. It was true to me—it had to be. For one thing, it clearly was rooted in that part of me that had always been different when it came to gender markers—all the way back to the shoe clerk, to my best friend in kindergarten.

For another thing, nothing of that power could be a simple misunderstanding. "Oops. Girl parts. Redirect!" It emanated from somewhere deep within me, and felt as though it touched every molecule in my body. It was, indeed, deeply and truly about me. And it was, indeed, deeply and truly about my feelings for Cathy. This dynamic young woman had been the object of my respect, awe, admiration, and affection since I first knew who she was. Star of our school musicals, with a powerful voice and charisma to spare, she had already rocked my world. I had arrived in this drab town the previous year following the death of my mother. I was a stranger here, alone and deep in grief. It felt to me that the very ground exuded pain. Cathy was a bright light. She loved music, was funny, and seemed fearless. Her personal mantra was the quote attributed to Helen Keller, "Life is a daring adventure or nothing at all." Cathy was *alive*. As I clawed my way out of the death chamber of my mother's mortality and all the loss it precipitated—home, family, community, school, friends—Cathy's energy was magnetic, vibrant, healing. She made me want to live.

All of that need, all of that desire crashed into me that day in Trig class. These feelings for Cathy were alive in every part of me—soul, mind, body. The sexual charge was a kind of resurrection that I hadn't even known to look for. I was in love. I was alive. A new way of understanding myself was emerging; a new identity was calling me forward. Life was taking me completely by surprise, and I had things to figure out, a hunger to satisfy. My first glimpse of my sexual identity was also bound up in this fierce need which was as much about my spirit as it was about my adolescent body: I was emerging from death to new life.

There is a great misconception that queerness is essentially about "who you sleep with."

People who think that their world would be easier if gay folk would just remain closeted might say that being queer is "only" about whom you sleep with. What is wrong with this notion is a lot, beginning with the disrespect it shows to the significance of sexual connection. But the problem is deeper than that: it ignores the fundamental importance not just of sex but also of sexual identity. Transgender experience is helpful here, with its focus less on "to whom I am drawn" and more on "who I am." It is not a stretch to grasp that one's sex is about much more than simply one's sexual organs.

Let's not kids ourselves. Whom you sleep with, like the sex of the body you inhabit, is enormously important. Sex is a drive, a force, of immense power. It is valuable, important, life giving—and can be, in its power, devaluing, dehumanizing, wounding, death dealing.

Those of us who may first have glimpsed a crucial piece of our identity as a sexual urge, as a longing for another with a decidedly (delightfully, terrifyingly) sexual component, we quickly had to grapple with the realization that more was at work than hormones and pheromones. I mean, hormones and pheromones were definitely at work, but there was also something more. Something caught up in that desire, shot through with desire, encompassing desire. Something that could not simply be turned off, or redirected to a more socially acceptable object of love and attraction.

I finished out high school nursing my love for Cathy, which was unrequited. She adored me and was an excellent friend with whom I did indeed share many daring adventures. My love for her was an important introduction to something inside of me. But while it is true that queerness is not "only" about whom you sleep with, it is also true that sex, the fleshy, liquid, orgasmic part, is for lots of people a pretty significant way to gauge whether or not an attraction is indeed an indicator of something deeper, of an identity. This did not happen to me until college. When it did, that was when I knew that my feelings were not a fluke, a trend, a phase, or an anomaly.

Okay, you should probably know something about me. I am not a little gay. I am completely gay. I am beyond completely gay. The Kinsey scale posits that sexual identity exists on a 6-point continuum, in which 0 is completely heterosexual and 6 is completely homosexual. On this scale, I am a 12.5.

This became perfectly clear to me when I engaged in my first relationship in which

I fell madly in love;
with someone who was in love with me;
and we had sex.

From the perspective that you may share as a human being who has experienced first love, you know about that one. It was the breakup that caused little stabbing sensations in my heart for, oh, about twenty-five years.

From my perspective as a person who is almost obsessive about examining and processing my inner world (hello, I'm a lesbian), this was when I began to perceive that being gay was more than simple shorthand for relational possibility. I rapidly came to see that being gay is a core identity marker for me. Meaning: It is one of those things I know about myself like I know my body. Like I know my name.

I am grateful for this knowledge. Identity markers, when you are in touch with them, are invaluable. Knowing who you are is an interior guide, a map, a directional force, an inner GPS system.

Being gay or some permutation of queer is a particularly interesting identity marker. It is not generally inherited (though sometimes it is). It may not connect you to anyone else in your family (though sometimes it does). It is a found identity, a discovered identity, a realized identity—both in the sense of being revealed and of being actualized, being made real. It emerges from within.

It is, in this sense, a spiritual identity. It is not handed over or known by kinship or tribe or ethnicity or residence or citizenship or race. It can be akin to religious identity, to creed, when that creed is adopted or realized in similar fashion. It is interior knowledge, existing within both psychic and physical planes. Comprising the totality of human identity—mind, spirit, body—sexual identity truly is knowledge of oneself. Or, at least, it makes knowledge available, if one chooses to pursue it, to explore it.

I love being a Southerner, love when I feel my Arkansas sensibility kicking in. I am also a New Yorker, who felt the draw of the city from a very young age and knew the moment I landed here that I had come home. The distinctive characters I count as ancestors, siblings, cousins make my familial identity quite visible to me. My political leanings, always progressive, have also been something of an identity marker. And of course my faith, powerfully experienced, has always been part of my essential makeup. All of these things I have known about myself for my entire conscious life.

Yet somehow it was my queerness that first taught me the clear connection between identity and ethics. It was in discerning my lesbianism, and my need of queer community, that I first perceived an identity that offered guidance, created obligations, helped push me out into the world to do work that I knew was important and necessary. This may have been largely the result of having to defend that identity in so many venues: personal, political, religious. Perhaps members of other communities, who face other kinds of identity-based pushback, also experience and will understand what I am describing. But regardless of the reason, this I know: It was my comprehension of queer identity that helped me first to comprehend my Christian identity. It was my comprehension of queer identity that helped me perceive the significance of Christianity as an identity marker at all. And this statement is particularly striking to me because, by the time I first really grasped the import of Christian identity, I had been working for years to articulate my identity as a priest. I had, in fact, already been ordained.

JANUARY 2008

I was serving as the Episcopal chaplain to Northwestern University. It was not my first professional ministry, but it was my first job as a priest. An instructor in Northwestern's Gender and Sexuality Studies Program asked me to guest lecture on Christian sexual ethics. As I prepared my presentation, I faced an immediate challenge: how to present my faith in a way that would be taken seriously by the students in this class. I knew that this would be a diverse crowd, probably including members of numerous faith traditions. I also knew there would be quite a few queer students. Interestingly, I felt confident that being gay would give me instant credibility, and that being a female/lesbian priest would at the very least be intriguing to some of the students. But I wanted something that would be harder for many of them: I wanted them to see what it was in my faith that I found so compelling. I wanted them to respect me as a Christian.

To do this, I needed them to be able to lay aside whatever prejudices and assumptions they carried around about the Christian tradition. I also wanted to approach the topic in a way that would not trigger wounds inflicted by the church on queer students—or any of the students—holding out the unlikely hope that an authentic read on the tradition might actually ease some of that pain. All of this led me to an inescapable conclusion: I had to start from square one, introducing the central tenets of Christianity as if the students had never heard anything about it at all. This needed to be more than a retelling of the gospel narrative. I needed to communicate what actually made visceral sense to me about this tradition: what it was that made me believe.

I found myself pondering the question that had so many times been posed to me by religious conservatives: "How do you know God doesn't condemn you as a lesbian?" Okay, I didn't actually ponder that question. I find that question to be a colossal waste of time. What I found myself pondering was my answer: "I know, because it's who I am." This is an answer that moves in two directions, expressing two truths simultaneously: I am gay, and I am caught up in this fantastic, passionate relationship with God—which I know, absolutely, to be reciprocal. These are not opinions, or postulates to a logical argument. They are truths, truths I perceive because both of them express something about me, about my soul, about my existence. Seeing myself so clearly—or more accurately, looking out at the world and feeling so unequivocally the ground of my perspective, I understand the power of identity. Pondering this, I recognized that this was also the answer to any challenge to my faith: "I believe, because it's who I am."

What I comprehended in that moment was much more than an answer to the question, "How do I explain my faith to others?" What I understood, more clearly than I ever had before, was what my faith meant to *me*. I saw that my faith isn't important to me because I am fascinated by the essential narrative of Christianity (although I am); rather, I am captivated by it because it expresses something that is going on inside me. No, that doesn't go far enough. It expresses something that is caught up in who I am. This is what I saw: in the same way that my lesbianism is built into the fiber of my being, so too are both my Christian faith and my priesthood built into the fiber of my being. Queerness, Christianity, priestliness—these exist inside of me, and I spend my daily life, my work, my relationships, finding ways to express what they reveal to me.

Suddenly I saw with fresh eyes the essence of what I have long known Jesus was trying to communicate to his contemporaries: "Put God first in your life. Orient your entire being toward the sacred. Not because I'm telling you that you should, not because it's what scripture tells you to do. Do it because *it's who you are*. It is who God made you to be." My lecture flowed easily from that point, as has every profession of faith I've made since.

Christian faith is premised on questions of identity. My tradition teaches that we are, first and foremost, God's creatures. God created us out of love, for the sheer joy of it. We are thus dependent on God for our very lives. We are inherently relational beings, created to love, existing in relationship with God and with one another. We have this tendency to run away from God, but God always comes after us. That's who God is: the One who loved us into being, who chooses us again and again; the One who always wants us back. That's who we are: objects of this passionate God's desire, and subjects who are able to stand consciously in relationship with this God, and with one another. We are creatures who have the power to choose God back.

That identity is the foundation upon which Christian theology, ethics, beliefs, and obligations of faith are built. The importance of identity was not an essentially Christian insight—we inherited it from the Israelite people, who recognized their identity as people created and chosen by God. But for Christians, identity becomes something that inexorably draws us into relationship with others across lines of ethnicity, nation, and social status. This is a transgressive movement that requires courage and demands risk.

CHAPTER 3

RISK

Let there be light.

—GOD

With this sentence, God sets in motion everything we know. Emerging from the traumatic events of the Babylonian exile, ancient Israelites drew on Mesopotamian and Egyptian myths to write the first chapters of what we now know as the book of Genesis. With stunning metaphor, these early theologians reassured their battered people of their place in God's heart. Creation emanates from within God, they wrote, as divine speech. We are the music God sings, the lyric that catches you by surprise when you find your deepest longing, your hardest loss, your most intense pleasure being sung aloud. Our universe is God's poem, intricate, sometimes cryptic, sometimes gritty, sometimes soaring with beauty, always alive, always being enunciated.

The myth of creation found in Hebrew scripture is designed to point us to truths about God, truths that are too difficult for our relative-to-God pea brains to comprehend fully, scientifically. The ancient Israelites, of course, were focused on a God whom they considered all-powerful, all-wise, all-knowing. For them, it was a revelation to contemplate the idea that this all-powerful God cared about creation, about us puny human beings. Conceiving the idea that God could actually love this creation, and call the Hebrew people—speaking personally to Abraham, to Moses —this was one of those moments when something changed for the human race. Right then, we evolved in our thinking. When you read scripture, both Hebrew and Greek, you always have to keep in the back of your mind the historical moments out of which these texts emerged, and the revolutionary ideas they were boldly proclaiming.

Several millennia later, those who read scripture bring other perspectives to bear. It is common today for people to feel that God is intimately bound up in our daily lives, to feel personally loved by this astonishing Spirit.

Viewing God that way, it is possible to wonder what creation was like for God. Not merely to assert, as the ancients did, that God viewed this creation favorably; but to imagine God wanting this creation, loving it, feeling both thrill and satisfaction when the stars began to glow, when that human creature's chest expanded with God's breath and . . . wait for it, wait . . . inhaled on hir own for the first time.

I have this vivid memory of my first child lying on a bed when he was just a few months old. He rolled over, for the first time. My reaction was amazement, delight, followed immediately by something almost akin to foreboding. My son was already a little perpetual motion machine, and now suddenly he would be able to get places on his own. I remember my exact thought: "Our lives have just changed completely, and forever."

Maybe the earliest moments of human agency were like that for God. God created us in Hir own image. We were part of God. And suddenly, we had our own power. We could think for ourselves where we wanted to go, and we could begin figuring out how to get there.

In order to create us, God took a risk. Not a small risk. A big risk. We don't know anything about what God had before then, so it's impossible to estimate the actual content of that risk. But it is safe to say this: God created us out of love. God had hope for us. And in a moment that may have compared to the ways that we risk for love, God put God's heart on the line for us.

Risk is what happens when you have something that you value and you take a chance with it, hoping to achieve something of greater value. Identity-based risks involve putting on the line something that is part of you, hoping to get a return on that investment that will also be part of you. These kinds of risks are particularly bracing, and particularly important. Scripture describes a God who models this exquisitely. Speaking creation into existence, breathing

Hir own life into it, God watches and waits to see what will happen next. What will we do? Where will we go? What risks will we take on behalf of love?

Not everyone in our various queer communities believes that queerness is a matter of identity. Queer theory argues that gender expression is less about identity and more about performance, and that gender is a construct.[1] This is important work, which addresses my simultaneous knowledge from childhood that I was a girl, and yet the qualities that people associate with "girlness"—the fashions, the demeanor—didn't fit me. Over the past thirty years, many people—from performance artists to philosophers to theologians—have pushed this insight further. They have so provocatively challenged societal attachments to these constructs as to suggest that the only way truly to rupture the binary of male and female is to dispense with them as essential categories—identity markers—at all. This is a foundational conversation in the art of queering, and there is no small liberation in it. When it becomes a conscious act, performance takes guts; especially when it bucks the tide of conventional perception or prescribed roles. It matters that we claim the power to choose how to present ourselves to the world—not just queer people, but all of us.

Numerous clerics inside Roman Catholicism have in recent years been lifting up what they call "gender theory," mischaracterizing academic conversations about gender and identity in stridently alarmist terms.[2] Even Pope Francis joined the fray, a discouraging move after his refreshing efforts to shine pastoral light into the dank spaces of LGBTQ exclusion.[3]

Such blatant fearmongering by religious conservatives merely strengthens the resolve to claim queerness itself as an identity marker. My experience tells me plainly that something deep is at work in the ways many of us make our sexual identities visible to the world. How we appear to the world is connected to something inside us. It is not merely "who I present myself to be," but is more truly "who I am."

Revealing oneself authentically always carries potential risk, however remote. Most human beings could tell stories not just about the risk of authenticity, but about times when they revealed themselves and were burned as a result. Many people, not just queer people, know what it is to risk something far greater than social embarrassment simply by walking down the street being who they are.

Queer people have a particular relationship to risk. Our need to be honest about our identities is not merely an ethical exercise. In order to find deep, intimate connection—which is to say, in order to love and be loved deeply, intimately—we have to reveal ourselves. This means that the stakes are high before we have even said a word.

Different kinds of queerness can entail very different levels of visibility. We often have some power to choose how we reveal ourselves, power that we exercise deliberately. Virtue is cultivated when one repeatedly chooses to step into a place of risk in order to live authentically into one's identity. For a trans* man, for instance, this may begin with a decision early in the discernment process to get a wicked short haircut and start wearing a tie. For a bisexual person, it may be the first time she openly confronts someone's casual assumption that the sex of the person she is with is a sweeping indicator of the kind of person she desires.

By living into our identities in any way whatsoever, we consciously enter a place of risk. Whatever that first risky step looks like, however cautiously modest, one thing is certain: at some point the risk will be grave, the danger real. The risks, the dangers, can be social, but they may also be—are very likely to be—physical, sexual, economic, emotional, legal, professional, familial, and most assuredly spiritual.

To live a queer life is to put oneself at risk—among family members, at work, on the street, and even in our homes. Telling the truth about queer identity takes courage. Embarking on the quest to find other queer people can be frightening, even perilous. If Christians understand and respect nothing else about queer experience, they should recognize this: proclaiming what you know to be true—especially in the face of hostility and ridicule—takes guts. Many queer people have a visceral understanding of Jesus's words, "Those who try to make their life secure will lose it. . . . For what will it profit them to gain the whole world and forfeit their life?"[4]

Nowhere do we walk the walk of faith more than in our quotidian decisions to live openly, visibly—on the streets, in our jobs, everywhere. Being out in a hostile world requires trust in something more important, and thus more secure, than physical safety. It may be a prioritization of one's identity—"I have to be who I am." It may come from a sense that it simply matters to tell the truth—a prioritization of one's integrity. And it may come from the knowledge that things will only change—for me, for all of us—by risking hits on ourselves individually as we witness to a larger truth: that our identities, our integrity, have value. This is rooted in the knowledge that one's truth is a part of a larger truth, and at some point this larger truth will win out.

This is fine to say—"Truth will win out in the end"—and I do honestly believe it. But that fine sentiment does not in any way diminish the hard fact that queer people take enormous risks simply by being ourselves in the world. And I don't just mean the occasional socially awkward moment. There are queer people who live in actual physical danger the world over.

In 2014 engaging in same-sex sexual activity was a criminal offense in more than seventy-five countries across the globe.[5] People convicted of violating these laws could be put to death in at least five countries, including the US ally nations of Saudi Arabia and Qatar. One nasty remnant of British colonialism is Section 377, an antisodomy law written into the penal codes of British-occupied states. More than thirty countries still have on the books either Section 377 or a law modeled on it, including Singapore, Pakistan, India, Bangladesh, and Jamaica.

The persistence of these laws is unnerving to queer people and our allies. In many countries these are not mere statutory relics of a bygone colonial era, but are actively enforced with severe consequences. Even in countries that do not criminalize homosexuality explicitly, such as Egypt, queer people have in recent years been prosecuted for "debauchery" or other vague charges.[6] The drumbeat of state-sponsored violence remains background noise in the lives of LGBTQ people across the globe, marching us backward from the progress that we have made in trying to build a more just and less violent world.

In one three-month span from December 2013 to February 2014, queer people were assailed by the following news items: The Supreme Court of India reaffirmed the constitutionality of India's

Section 377, overturning a 2009 ruling that had decriminalized homosexuality, and "once again making gay sex a crime punishable by up to ten years in jail and putting tens of millions of Indians at risk of prosecution or harassment."[7] The Olympic Games in Sochi drew international attention to a then-recent Russian law that criminalized alleged pro-LGBTQ propaganda. And these headlines appeared in international news sources: "Museveni Says He Plans to Sign Anti-Gay Law after All";[8] "Wielding Whip and a Hard New Law, Nigeria Tries to 'Sanitize' Itself of Gays";[9] and "Mob Attacks More Than a Dozen Gay Men in Nigeria's Capital."[10]

For queer Christians, the queerphobic laws in Uganda and Nigeria particularly sting. This is partly because the Ugandan law that passed in 2013 was so draconian, partly because Uganda was at one time considered a model success story in the fight to stem HIV/AIDS, and largely because the laws were supported by so many religious leaders, including the Anglican archbishops in both countries. These archbishops had taken highly visible leadership roles excoriating the Episcopal Church in the United States for consecrating Gene Robinson as its first openly gay bishop in 2003. The rift in the Anglican Communion threatened to become a schism. The archbishop of Nigeria at the time was scathing in his indictment of any notion of a queer-tolerant Christianity, asserting that the ordination of openly gay priests is "an idea sponsored by Satan himself and being executed by his followers and adherents who have infiltrated the church."[11]

We do not have to look to nonwestern nations for constant news of queerphobic assaults. The New York City Anti-Violence Project (AVP), which works to prevent and respond to violence against and within queer and HIV-affected communities in New York, charts these crimes on a continuous basis. On August 17, 2013, Islan Nettles, a trans* woman of color, was beaten to death in central Harlem. On May 17, 2013, Mark Carson, an openly gay man, was shot and killed in Greenwich Village, surely one of the most gay-friendly neighborhoods in the world.

These laws and attacks got a lot of attention when they were first reported, but they were not new then, and they are not unusual. What is shocking is that for all the change we have seen, for all the movement on legal and social fronts, we don't seem to make a dent in curbing the violence being perpetrated against LGBTQ people.

Catherine Shugrue dos Santos is the director of client services at AVP and deeply sensitive to the ways violence can be amplified against people who face multiple forms of bias. "As a queer person, I know what it's like to be afraid of rejection, or even for my safety because of who I am," she recently stated. "But as a White cisgender woman, I have to be honest with myself and admit that I don't know how I would handle the amount of violence directed, for instance, at trans* women of color. I'm not talking about discomfort. I'm talking about actual physical danger. Think of how much safety planning has to go into the simplest daily activity, like walking to get groceries."

The danger is real. In 2012 the National Coalition of Anti-Violence Programs (NCAVP) documented more than two thousand incidents of hate violence against LGBTQ people in the United States. Transgender women were twice as likely to experience discrimination, threats, and intimidation as survivors who did not identify as transgender women, and transgender women of color were nearly three times as likely to experience police violence compared to white cisgender survivors.[12]

Shugrue dos Santos reminds us that it is a privileged idea that "safety is normal." And not just on the streets. Of hate violence reported to the NCAVP, the highest number of incidents are those perpetrated by landlords, tenants, or neighbors. Second highest are those perpetrated by employers or coworkers.[13] Safety is indeed not normal, not for the vast majority of people in the world, and certainly not for most queer people—not even in our homes and workplaces.

Christianity takes dead aim at the impulse to amass power and privilege in pursuit of security, a concept that includes personal safety. This is partly for spiritual reasons—Christians are taught to rely on God, not on our stuff, for safety. But Christianity also recognizes that there is a reciprocal relationship between the quest for privilege and the inequality that breeds unsafe conditions for everyone. While gated communities may tempt their inhabitants into insidious spiritual complacency, the wealth that is being guarded there also saps resources from those who live outside the gates. The Christian gospel thus recognizes that privilege run amok actually makes most people less safe than they might be in a more economically just society. This is true for LGBTQ people, but it is also true for young men of color, women of all ages, children in the developing world—everyone, really, who is not cloistered behind those gates.

No authentic read of Christianity can fail to comprehend the tradition's analysis of these economic dynamics. But the tradition does not stop at economics when making truth claims about our safety and security. Christianity also recognizes the degree to which spiritual fears make people unsafe.

It sickens me how effectively fear of sexual difference continues to be used as a weapon against my people. This is a deep and disturbing spiritual malaise that afflicts not only perpetrators of violence, but also and far more heartbreakingly the people who find themselves in its crosshairs. In 2011 Michael Bacon, a priest, began to compile news reports of young people who had killed themselves, or tried to, because they were being bullied. Within a few weeks, Michael had uncovered approximately seventy accounts of youth suicides in countries across the globe. Thirty-five were reported in the press to be gay. He found multiple instances of girls killing themselves as couples. It is not a surprise, though it should be, that several of the news accounts included explicit reference to religious-based taunts, or worse, queerphobic quotes from local pastors.

Given the role that spiritual violence plays in the decisions of these young people to end their lives, it is fair to ask why progressive churches are not doing more to prevent their deaths. The need is real, and it is urgent.

Ignoring the roots of such violence leaves a shameful and lasting record, one that can be seen clearly in other historical moments. For example, in 2015 the Equal Justice Initiative issued a report that documented nearly four thousand racial terror lynchings in the United States from 1877 to 1950.[14] The report gained widespread press attention when it was released, not just because the numbers were much higher than had been previously documented, but also because the authors characterized these lynchings as a form of terrorism against African Americans. The threat of lynching, the report notes, led to the "forced migration of millions of black Americans out of the South."

The report asserts that most terror lynchings had one or more common features, the first of which is "a wildly distorted fear of interracial sex."[15] Which is to say, terror lynchings depended upon and deliberately ignited white society's fear of the rupturing of racial and sexual binaries that were built into Southern power structures and designed to maintain white dominance.

The national tide that finally turned against lynching was led by people of diverse races,[16] mostly Christians whose disgust at lynching was informed by their religious convictions. The most active white-led organization, the Association of Southern Women for the Prevention of Lynching, was organized specifically to rebut and condemn the lie that lynching was perpetrated in order to "protect" Southern women. But white Christian antilynching efforts stopped short of confronting the troubling correlation between rural evangelical Christianity and rural lynching,[17] nor did they challenge "the narrative of racial difference that is the most enduring evil of American slavery."[18]

For some in the 1930s, the decision not to challenge pernicious racial binaries was a calculated move to advance important political ends. But by failing to proclaim a Gospel that would confront and dismantle the conceptual underpinnings of racial terrorism, Christian leaders ceded the most potent instrument of their moral authority. The legacy of this theological vacuum continues to affect people's real lives, disturbingly, to this day.

The violence directed at queer people differs substantially from the reign of racial terror that fueled an African American exodus from the American South. In the United States, there is nothing in queer experience that compares to the moral abomination that was the institution of slavery, to the terror that it bred, and to its legacy of dehumanizing violence.

The weapons against queer people differ not just in scale from those used in acts of racial terror, but also in method. Because we are seldom born into queer families, many of us spend years alone before we find queer community. Those who would terrorize us have thus crafted weapons that pick us off individually before we have found our people. Though queer people certainly are forced to deal with external threats of violence, the terrorism directed at us relies heavily on weapons that we ingest with our minds, hearts, and souls. They are spiritual weapons. Delivered relentlessly over a course of years, these weapons prove to be so spiritually corrosive that many queer people take their own lives to escape the inflicted pain and internalized shame. Some queer youth do indeed flee north, or west, to find safe harbors in urban centers with large LGBTQ communities. But others simply flee the world that has bullied them relentlessly and condemned them as evil.

This is terrorism at work. It is spiritual terrorism, and the voices that are most urgently needed to combat this terrorism are the voices of religious authority.

It is good for churches to be inclusive of queer people, but it is not enough. It is important for clergy to be pastoral to queer people, but it is not enough. What is needed now is a bold, pastoral, explicitly Christian response that does what white antilynching activists were not willing to do with regards to race: rupture the false binaries that are employed to demonize queer identity. It matters that we preach not only that the violence is wrong and anti-Christian, but also *why* it is wrong and anti-Christian.

Having named those deadly binaries, explicitly, as an affront to the queer God whom we Christians worship, we must then create liturgical moments that honor the lives of queer people—those who have survived, and those who have not. Michael Bacon's spiritual community determined that it would mark the deaths he had uncovered with prayer and vigil. He created a binder with photos of these young people, telling their stories. Paging through it is an exercise in heartbreak. His community used the visual presentations as the centerpiece of a month-long series of masses, concluding with a requiem. I attended this requiem and will not forget it. Bacon's words reverberate still: "To each gay child or youth who has taken his/her life, let us not say, 'Rest in peace.' Let us say, 'Our rage at your fate remains undiminished; our prayer is that in the other place you live the life of which you were deprived here, one of fullness, joy, and love.'"

My queer identity is a source of such immense joy for me that I almost can't comprehend how it could lead to suicidal self-hatred. And yet, of course I understand it. I understand it completely. All you have to do is stop tuning out the background noise of violence and listen, simply listen, to the violently queerphobic words on the lips of people who bear the mantle of spiritual authority.

When you listen, what becomes truly amazing is that any of us ever come out at all. And yet we do, in waves that have gotten stronger and stronger, throughout the entire world.

Why do we do this?? Why do we persist in telling our truth? Why would anyone choose to put themselves in the path of bullying, of professional danger, of familial rejection, of assault on the street? Why do we go to the lengths we do, making the safety plans, enduring the taunts, tuning *in* the headlines and organizing to make this world a place where we are able not just to live but fabulously shine?

Well, why *do* we do it? I believe that the answer is tied up in another deeply theological concept: hope. Hope is vital to the human heart, and it matters to understand what it is, and what it isn't.

When I graduated from seminary, I landed a job as chaplain to the AIDS Health Services unit at Jersey City Medical Center in Jersey City, New Jersey. This was 1991, the height of the AIDS pandemic in the United States. There were no drug cocktails that kept opportunistic infections at bay. An HIV diagnosis back then meant that death was almost certainly around the corner. Jersey City had the highest rate of HIV infection in the country for a city its size, and Medical Center was deep in the inner city. In the four years that I worked there, more than six hundred people in our service died. Children, women, men. Black, white, brown.

Death from HIV/AIDS was like nothing I had seen before, or since. If allowed to run rampant, the virus wipes out a body's immune system, thwarting its ability to fight germs that would be turned away at the gate by healthy, well-armed immunities. Back then we watched helplessly as infection after infection took hold. None who were on the front lines as patients, survivors, and professional caregivers will ever forget the sights and smells of human decay that we witnessed. This was especially true for those of us who served inner-city patients, whose decline was often intensified by a raft of other poverty-related complications. But neither,

I suspect, will any of us ever forget the moments of stunning human dignity displayed by people who refused to let the disease be all that defined them.

One of the patients I met in the hospital was Celia, a young Latina woman. She arrived early in her battle with HIV. When I met her in her hospital room, she was sick but attractive, articulate, and filled with life. She told me that she had recently joined an evangelical church. The folks in this community had stepped up to provide considerable support to Celia and her family. In my experience in the hospital, this was a rarity. I hardly ever ran into members of the clergy visiting my patients. I suspected that this was a mutual decision: clergy didn't want to visit my patients, but they weren't necessarily welcome, either. The vast majority of my patients who belonged to a church at some point in their lives had eventually been burned by it. Local congregations had little interest in serving gay men, and less interest in serving folks involved in the IV drug culture that was savaging their neighborhoods.

I was intrigued by Celia's experience being embraced in this church. She and I talked at length. What became apparent was that the church had taken her on as something of a test case. They were determined to heal her of her HIV infection through prayer. Given how vibrant she was, I could easily imagine their thinking: "If anyone can be cured, she can."

In our conversations, Celia talked about hope. She still had big dreams for her life, so when she used the word "hope," she meant a lot of things: hope that she would live a long life, hope that she would do work that was valuable, hope that her life would have meaning. What gradually became clear was that the folks in her church defined "hope" as something much more specific: hope that Celia would one day test HIV negative.

Over the course of months, Celia's immune system began to crash. As she got sicker, members of her church began to peel away. She kept her chin up, refusing to disparage these people for abandoning her. Our work together took a deeper and harder turn as she grappled with her sense that she had failed, that she had let these people down. We were still talking about hope, and the challenge before me was daunting. Could I help Celia unshackle herself from the narrow definition of hope imposed on her by this church?

How do you talk about hope with someone who is dying? What is hope, anyway? What can any of us reasonably hope for in this life?

When Celia told me that she had finally accepted that her hope was unrealistic, I hit a wall. The one thing I believed about hope, the one thing I knew absolutely to be true, was that "hope" and "real" do not and cannot stand opposed to each other. A person may wish for things that don't come to fruition, but "hope" exists. By definition, there is no such thing as "false hope."

The question of hope was something that virtually every single one of my patients was wrestling with at some level. So I prayed for understanding. I studied scripture. I listened carefully to my patients. I talked at length with the nuns and priests and other caregivers who were my colleagues in AIDS ministry.

The answer came from an unexpected source. I went to see Frank Darabont's film adaptation of Stephen King's novella *The Shawshank Redemption*. There is this moment when Andy, the character played by Tim Robbins, commandeers the warden's office to broadcast an aria over the prison's PA system. Movement in the yard stops as prisoners look up and listen. For a moment you can see the men transported beyond the walls. Andy gets two weeks in solitary for the stunt. When he gets out, he tells other inmates that he survived it by listening internally to a Mozart piece that he knew by heart. He asks if any of them use music in that way. Red, played by Morgan Freeman, scoffs at him. The derision takes Andy by surprise. He struggles to articulate what he means. "You need [music] so you don't forget that there's something inside they can't get to, that they can't touch, that's yours." Red asks warily, "What are you talking about?" Andy looks him in the eye. "Hope."

I knew instantly that this was what I'd been struggling to grasp. Hope for these prisoners wasn't that they would one day get out. It was the knowledge that some part of them wasn't locked up. For my patients, true hope wasn't the possibility that someday they would be cured; it was the knowledge that some part of them wasn't sick.

I wish I could tell you that I brought this insight to Celia and she immediately got it, that her decline from there on out was a peaceful one, that she died with a level of spiritual freedom. But my memory is that she sort of faded away after the folks in that church gave up on her. Once a religious community steps in to tell you what to believe about yourself, what to hope for, what hope *is*, it is very hard to put those ideas down. This is one of the most important reasons that the rallying cry for LGBTQ people is "Pride," a concept that is shot through with hope. We long ago learned to stop listening to the disparaging messages being pounded into us by folks with religious authority. We learned to claim the authority to tell the truth about ourselves, and we learned to celebrate our identities as both valid and valuable.

When a queer person comes out—that is, tells the truth of her life—that person is living into hope. Whatever risk she takes, she has to believe that some part of her will survive whatever happens next, that some part of her is stronger than the hate and the intimidation and the violence.

Risk taking can be a form of thrill seeking, but that's not the kind of risk I'm talking about now. I'm not talking about recklessness, either. I'm talking about the kind of risk you take because you are caught up in truth, and you simply have to trust it, tell it, live into it. That's the essence of faith—trusting in something that you know to be true. Solidly true. True in a way that is both inside you and bigger than you. You see, faith isn't trust in the idea that you will be safe (that "safety is normal," as Shugrue dos Santos says). It is trust in the idea that some part of you—the truth in you—will survive no matter what death-dealing violence is directed at you.

This kind of risk is the verb form of faith. It is the lived iteration of trust in something bigger than your immediate security, bigger than whatever threat exists to your security. Risk isn't just a by-product, an inevitable consequence of actions that push you out of a comfortable zone. It is the means itself, the requisite stuff, the fuel, the essence.

Queer people may not always understand risk this way, but Christians must. For queer people it can be as much a source of terror as of joy. But for Christians, this kind of risk is part and parcel of love, which is the primary impulse, purpose, and mission of our tradition; of the God whom we worship. It is where we locate our hope, a hope that "does not disappoint us," as Paul says;[19] a hope that never fails.

We Christians talk about God as love. We talk about love as the glue that holds our community together, that identifies us to the world. Yet one seldom sees in a church anything approaching the risks that queer people take every day for the sake of love. When Christians do offer this kind of witness, the power of authentic Christianity becomes immediately visible even to secular observers. In June 2015 leaders of the historically black Emanuel AME Church in Charleston, South Carolina, welcomed a stranger, a young white man, and engaged him in dialogue about scripture. As he began to spew racist invective and pulled a gun, they met his hateful violence with love and courage.

In his eulogy for Emanuel's pastor, the Reverend Clementa Pinckney, President Obama eloquently described this encounter and the impact it had on people who heard the story. "Blinded by hatred, the alleged killer could not see the grace surrounding Reverend Pinckney and that Bible study group—the light of love that shone as they opened the church doors and invited a stranger to join in their prayer circle. The alleged killer could never have anticipated the way the families of the fallen would respond when they saw him in court—in the midst of unspeakable grief, with words of forgiveness. . . . The alleged killer could not imagine how the city of Charleston . . . how the state of South Carolina, how the United States of America would respond—not merely with revulsion at his evil act, but with big-hearted generosity and, more importantly, with a thoughtful introspection and self-examination that we so rarely see in public life."[20]

Many factors played a role in the public introspection and self-examination that the president describes, but perhaps the most significant was simply the integrity and courage shown by the people of this church *as* a church. "Emanuel does not harbor hate in her heart," the sister of one victim was quoted as saying. "That's not the God we serve."[21] The people of this church witnessed to their faith in such a God: faith that demands material risk that is qualitatively similar to the risks that queer people take on a daily basis throughout the world.

Queer people risk in this way for ourselves, but we also do it for one another. Like the people of Emanuel Church and so many others involved in movements toward justice, we do it because we know that the only way not to be crushed by persecution is to recognize that our connection to one another paves the road to our survival. It is the way we may someday establish a better, more just world, but it also allows those of us who are killed to live on. And so we risk, knowing that we are part of a life, a love, a truth, that cannot die.

This is a complex way of understanding what safety is, because it stands on its head the conventional notion that security is about making your body safe. This is an inversion, in which "security" is best achieved by putting yourself at risk. It is more than an inversion: it is the rupturing of a binary in which "safety" and "risk" stand in opposition to each other.

And this particular rupturing, this queering, exists at the heart of the Judeo-Christian tradition. The entire multimillennial history of both Judaism and Christianity comes back again and again to make the point that true security rests in our reliance on God alone. Indeed, these traditions grapple almost obsessively with the human temptation to forego reliance on God in favor of reliance on something—someone, some weapon, some empire—other than God. Virtually the entire canon of history and prophecy in Hebrew scripture and the entire narrative of Jesus's life, death, and resurrection is a sustained meditation on this very theme: reliance on God makes possible justice, love, life; while failure to rely on God—which is to say, fear of relying on God—breeds injustice, enmity, and death.

Am I equating reliance on God with the queer impulse to tell the truth about one's identity, to walk the streets being who one is, even in the face of intimidation and violence? You bet I am. This business of perceiving yourself caught up in a truth that exists inside you and is bigger than you—that is the essence of what it is to rely on God, to know God, to live in the thrall of God's astonishing, transgressive power. This is not to say that queer identity is the same thing as the identity of being God's creature. Clearly there are lots of people who are God's creatures who are not queer. It *is* to say that risking for the sake of truth is a sacred enterprise, and one can risk in this way for many reasons of which queerness is most assuredly one.

Queer virtue is a path that begins with discernment of an identity. Taking the risk to speak our identities out loud is the next crucial step on that path. It is a step that most of us, perhaps all of us, take over and over again. Coming out never ends. At the same time, this path is one that you get better at. If this is a step you have not taken, if you are still in a place where the fear or the danger is still just too great, I can promise you this: it does get easier the more you practice, the more you live openly as part of your daily life. I count myself blessed to live in New York, to work in a politically progressive office, to have the support of my church and my bishop. All of this has made it so much easier to be myself. My life has not always been like this. Many of us—perhaps most of us—have paid terrible prices for our honesty along the way. The ease of so many of our lives now is bolstered by the years we have spent paving roads, building spaces and relationships that afford a measure of safety. It really pays off. At this point in my life I am so accustomed to being out that I can't remember the last time I indicated to someone that I was gay and was conscious of doing so.[22]

But even if coming out is now pretty much de rigueur for me, queering—in the sense of rupturing binaries—is not. That I still have to do intentionally most of the time. It is not always easy; it is not always comfortable; and it sometimes involves terrifying risk. For good reason. Queering is itself dangerous, pushing people out of conventional comfort zones. I was recently reminded that in my childhood, the term "transgressive" would have indicated not something thrilling, but something dangerous, taboo, and even illegal. Fifty years ago, right here in the United States, people who challenged those big binaries—male/female, black/white, communist/capitalist—were widely considered to be criminals. The dangers they faced were often imposed by the police and court system, as well as by a disparaging society.

There have always been religious leaders who recognized that the impulse to question binaries is embedded in an authentic read of the Christian tradition. So it is both sad and ironic that the danger to those who queer today often emanates from people claiming to espouse or defend Christian faith.

Here's an example of deciding, intentionally, to queer something in the church.

Back in 2013 I was scheduled to preach at what was then my home church, All Saints Episcopal Parish in Hoboken, New Jersey. In the Episcopal Church, we follow a lectionary, a three-year cycle of biblical readings. When you agree to preach on a given Sunday, you are handed four biblical texts: one from Hebrew scripture, a Psalm, an Epistle, and one of the Gospels. The sermon is usually a reflection on one or more of these assigned readings. On this particular Sunday the gospel passage was Jesus and his mother at the wedding in Cana.[23] In the Episcopal wedding liturgy for heterosexual couples the priest begins by saying that "our Lord Jesus Christ adorned this manner of life by his presence and first miracle at a wedding in Cana of Galilee." Now, if you ask me, it's a bit of a stretch to say that just because Jesus was at this wedding, he intended his presence to be a permanent endorsement of the institution of marriage. If he had actually gotten married, it would be more persuasive. He didn't, at least not that we're aware of. The point is that I had avoided this text for years because of its association with a sacrament that until recently had been completely off limits to LGBTQ people. Finally, that Sunday, I decided to take it on.

As I started working with the text, I saw something amazing going on, something that had nothing to do with weddings, heterosexual or otherwise. What I saw was Jesus taking these pots of water—water designed for ritual bathing, for spiritual cleansing—and turning that water into wine that everyone was supposed to drink. What I saw was Jesus taking this substance that was all caught up in ideas of cleanness and uncleanness, all caught up in notions about what separates us from each other, and turning it into something designed to be shared, something that eases our anxiety about all the harsh lines in our world, something we take into our bodies in order to overcome barriers like ritual purity laws that separate us from one another.

What I saw was Jesus queering those pots of water.

So that became my sermon: a queer reading of the wedding at Cana. I was so deliciously intoxicated by the queering in this story that I knew I had to be explicit about it. And I also knew that there would be lots of churches where a sermon like that would get me fired. I was pretty sure that I would not get fired at All Saints, because I was 100 percent certain that my boss, Geoff Curtiss, would have my back. Even so, when I ran into him in the sacristy that morning the first thing I said was, "Geoff, I would like to apologize up front for the guff you are going to take for the sermon I am about to preach." Geoff laughed. He taught me a lot that day about the role that straight allies can play in giving cover to us queerfolk as we do this radical, unpredictable work of queering.

Because we need cover for this. Simply naming our perspective as "queer" is more than a lot of parishioners can handle. One of the easiest ways that progressive denominations could ignite interest in the binary-busting aspects of Christian theology would be to free up queer clergy to proclaim the Gospel from an explicitly queer perspective, boldly and honestly. Let us be ourselves, and assure us that you will have our backs when our proclamation unsettles and afflicts those who are comfortable in a dualistic worldview.

Queering itself is risky business. To reject easy binaries is to enter into uncertain terrain. The discomfort of such liminal space is often at the heart of the fear that erupts in violence against queer people—violence that may be physical, or legal, or ecclesial, or economic. You really can get fired for it, even in denominations that pride themselves on being gay friendly.[24] Lots of priests and pastors have.

And that's just so many shades of wrong, because in fact, busting those false dichotomies is part and parcel of the Judeo-Christian tradition. It is one of the bedrock reasons I am a Christian and love my tradition so much. Christianity pushes me right off that cliff of comfortable binaries all the time, and I need that. It is sometimes ridiculously hard, and egregiously painful, and sometimes it simply pisses me off. "Love my enemy? Do good to those who persecute us? How could love and persecution possibly coexist??"

The Judeo-Christian Bible begins with a mythic account of creation. Out of the realm of heaven, beyond time and space, God speaks the created order into existence. Something of immense power passes back and forth between, among these realities of time and space, and since it began, it has never stopped. If you have ever truly prayed, truly meditated, casting aside your firm grip on your solid existence, you know. If you have ever found yourself transported to another dimension by an extraordinary piece of music, you know. However you got there, whatever has carried you there, if you have ever let yourself enter that other place of reality, you know: It exists, and we have access to it. It has access to us.

This is how the myth of creation starts. Then the Bible tells the story of God's relationship with the Hebrew people. The entire narrative of our faith begins with God calling Abraham to leave his home and all that he knows in search of something, he knows not what. A millennium or so later the apostle Paul points to Abraham's risk-taking faith as a model for future generations. Abraham risks everything, says Paul, "being fully convinced that God was able to do what [God] had promised. Therefore his faith 'was reckoned to him as righteousness.'"[25]

It matters that we understand what it is that Abraham gets right here. Or rather, it matters not to misunderstand. A lot of people think that Abraham models blind obedience to God. That is a misinterpretation that then gets carried into one of the hardest stories in scripture: Abraham's near sacrifice of his son, Isaac.[26] God tells Abraham to sacrifice Isaac, and Abraham unquestioningly prepares to do just that. The dramatic tension builds and builds as we wait to see whether Abraham is actually going to do this dreadful thing. At the very last moment, with Abraham grasping the knife, poised to plunge it into Isaac's small body, an angel steps in to grab Abraham's arm. People of good conscience for generations have struggled with this story's meaning. Many people sensitive to the plight of abused children recoil in horror at the idea of God pitting Abraham against Isaac in this way.

Theologian and Old Testament scholar Walter Brueggemann argues that the message of this story has nothing to do with obedience—especially obedience to what appears to be an arbitrarily violent God. The message here is that Abraham has already come to trust God so thoroughly that Abraham knows instinctively that something else is afoot. Brueggemann locates in this story the first human inkling of resurrection.

"Resurrection concerns the keeping of a promise when there is no ground for it," Brueggemann writes. "Faith is nothing other than trust in the power of the resurrection against every deathly circumstance. Abraham knows beyond understanding that God will find a way to bring life even in this scenario of death."[27]

The story of Abraham lays the groundwork for the most fundamental elements of what will become both the Christian narrative and the Christian faith. It all centers on the boldest claim that human beings can make: that there is something at work that is bigger than we are, and the essence of that something is bound up in love. What it requires of us, first and foremost, is a willingness to demonstrate our perception of that love—our faith in that love—by diving headlong, again and again, into the potent mix of risk and trust.

People struggling under the weight of oppression have long recognized that God is not to be found in the taskmaster who holds the whip. Rather, God is found in the long arc "that bends toward justice," as Martin Luther King Jr. said.[28] When people who claim to be following Jesus participate in holding that whip, against any group, something is very, very wrong. It is a violation of everything we Christians profess to believe. Our call is to risk unknown consequences in pursuit of what we are supposed to know beyond understanding: that God will bring life, even in scenarios that challenge us to our core. That call does not end—in fact, it becomes more demanding—when one wields power over the lives and well-being of others.

It is not a surprise that LGBTQ communities have made such progress establishing moral credibility while growing numbers of people have simultaneously dismissed Christian authority as hypocritical and hollow. If you open your eyes to see a young person doing the bold work of naming hir sexual identity, and you observe a person "of faith" holding a spiritual knife over that young person's soul, it is impossible not to see that the young person is doing what the church is supposed to be doing: trusting, risking, for the sake of love. This is exactly the moment when the church is supposed to hear the voice of God saying, "Put the knife down. This child is innocent." If this is a test, it is not a test of the child. Nor, I am convinced, is it a test to see if people of faith will cling rigidly to a few obscure passages of scripture. If it is a test, it is a test of faith, and far too many Christians are failing it.

It is true that LGBTQ communities have struggled mightily with the impulse to keep certain members down, invisible, for fear of compromising our overall progress or our individual security. Our work is not complete. An honest person recognizes that it never will be complete, at least not in human time. What LGBTQ people have going for us is that we have long had prophets of extraordinary moral courage in our ranks, prophets who try to pay attention not just to our sexual identities, but also to other particularities that afford privilege or exact vulnerability. One sees that courage clearly on display in the stories of people like Caleb Orozco of Belize, who has endured assault and death threats for working to overturn his country's law that criminalizes same-sex sexual activity. Or David Kato, an openly gay African man and founder of Sexual Minorities Uganda (SMUG) who was murdered in his home on January 26, 2011. Or in the prophetic witness of our allies the Reverend John Makokha and his wife, Anne Baraza, who run Other Sheep Afrika-Kenya, an LGBTI ecumenical organization that preaches openly and honestly about the African male sex industry, religious homophobia and transphobia, social injustice, and HIV/AIDS. Americans Laverne Cox, Janet Mock, and Caitlyn Jenner have used their success and the global influence of the US media to tell their stories, boldly building awareness and understanding of trans* identity. Our prophets include people who are famous, and people who live next door. They are the countless activists who have refused to be invisible and silent in India, Russia, Brunei, Egypt, Britain, the United States, or . . . just spin the globe and let your finger drop on a country that is crucifying its queer children.

Look around. The courage is breathtaking. But honestly, nowhere does one see acts of voluntary, intentional, courageous risking like those demonstrated by God Hirself. This is what God models to us by creating the universe at all, by creating us, creatures in Hir own image, with agency to love God back—or not. God doesn't just set up some arbitrary rule for us: "Risk is the verb form of faith. I demand this of you!" No, God lives this. God risks Godself in order to connect to us, God's creatures. Christianity asserts that God goes even further, showing up as an infant. Talk about risk. That baby is risk incarnate.

Why does God do this?

To try to glimpse the answer, we have to dig deeper. Scary and dangerous as risking is, it is not an end in itself. Not for God, not for us. Risk is the means to the even scarier, more dangerous, and ultimately more desirable end: the ability to connect with others, the ability to touch and be touched.

CHAPTER 4

TOUCH

*I know you are reading this poem which is not in your language
guessing at some words while others keep you reading
and I want to know which words they are.*

—ADRIENNE RICH

The intimacy of these lines traces something deep and hungry and erotic in me. They run a finger along my enfleshed soul, my ensouled body, stirring a craving for something I can barely name.

I want.

I want to be touched in this way.

I want someone to reach for me, to reach from inside her own perception, her own feeling, her own need. I want to feel her stir next to me, as a lover turns in the dark blue night to face me with her entire body, bury her face in the skin of my back, the palm of her hand traveling from my hip to my stomach to my chest. She holds me there, knows me, wants me, needs me. I want this and need this, too: the power of this connection, this touch.

When one's identity is caught up in one's sexuality, it is not a stretch to perceive the erotic at work as it courses through our lives.[1] I don't mean physical sex, necessarily; I mean the underlying electric current that connects people intimately, and that connects human beings to God.

The desire for this electric charge—palpable, sensual, spiritual—is what leads me to risk. My need of it is so great that I'm not sure I could not pursue it. But if I had a choice about the matter, if I could choose whether or not to pursue the erotic desire for deep connection, I know that I would choose it. Absolutely. This desire is very like my queerness in that regard: something built into me, something I love. Something I want, even as I know that it is itself the essence of wanting.

The human species has a long history of ambivalence about the value both of bodies and of desire. By "ambivalence," what I mean is that it is possible to trace through many cultures, philosophies, and theologies a near demonization of flesh and of desire. And sometimes that demonization isn't just "near." Sometimes it is explicit, and deadly. It's not hard at all to see disparagement of bodies and fear of desire undergirding sexual violence the world over—against women, against people of color, against children, against queer people.

When queer people begin to live openly, when we make our queerness visible, we take on both aspects of this demonization. That need to live openly is born of desires that are hard for a healthy individual to repress, that a healthy individual knows in his gut he should not repress: desire for connection, desire for authenticity, desire for pleasure, desire for human dignity. And of course, that desire is located intimately in our bodies.

Life is a struggle for most of us, in some ways for all of us, queer or not. You have to want simply to survive, and you have to put some energy behind that wanting if you are going to do more than survive. For the vast majority of people, just getting one's basic needs met can feel like a long trudge up a steep hill. I once heard someone describe the amount of privilege you have as being like your position on that hill. If you have a good life, a loving family, a level of material comfort, you don't have to trudge so far to live well. But for every challenge handed to you, you start a little lower down the hill. If you live in poverty, or in the midst of violence, or if your tribe/gender/racial or ethnic group is disparaged in some way, those facts put you a few notches down. The further down the hill you are, the more grit you have to have to get your needs met, let alone to succeed beyond that.

The image of this hill is compelling. All by itself it makes me skeptical of theologies that posit desire as somehow problematic, or worse, as sinful. There is no question that for many, many people in the world, desire for life is what keeps you, your family, your children, alive. Wanting to live, wanting a better life, keeps people walking up that hill. Not only does this desire, this drive, make sense, but it is clearly valuable, honorable. Maybe this is why so many queer people have no trouble extending a basic acceptance of desire to include the desires that define so much of who we are.

Many queer people want. Openly. We have to want openly if we are to get the things we want and need. What queer people want is probably not a lot different from what most people want: connection, meaning, safe harbors, belonging. Love. What is different about us is that we are marked by these desires in a way many other people are not marked. And we are marked by a very specific aspect of those desires: many of them are carnal. They involve our bodies. They are about sex, whether as identifier, or physiological phenomenon, or activity.

Some queer people pay less attention to the implications of embodiment, but many of us are fiercely carnal—and aware of it. We have to be aware of it, because our carnality commands so much attention, infuses so many conversations about our lives. Our carnality is *the* subject that people discuss when they talk about "the issue" of who we are. This fact alone distinguishes queer carnality from heterosexual embodiment. What is extraordinary, breathtaking, is the degree to which we as a people have boldly claimed our carnality. In our various communities, we celebrate it. We take pride in it.

But something more. Something important. Even as queer communities have paid careful attention to bodies and sex, we have also paid careful attention to spiritual health, to our inherent human dignity and integrity. We have had to do this, in a world that all too often pits body against spirit in dualistic, antagonistic tension. We have had to do this, because we want. Because wanting itself is so often a deeply spiritual impulse.

That is what many of us experience in our queerness, and in our spirituality. They work together. They overlap, intermingle. Part of the premise of this book is that being queer has taught me a lot about how to be a good Christian. But it does sometimes go the other way, that my faith tradition helps me understand my queerness.

Contemporary Christianity has expended so much wattage on disparagement of bodies and of desire that most people probably take it as a given that this disparagement of flesh, of wanting, is a bright thread in the history of the tradition. But Christianity has

always celebrated desire for God, even fierce desire of that electri-
cally charged (yes, I'm going to say it) erotic variety. Now don't
let that word sidetrack our conversation. I'm not going to get all
defensive here and tell you that by "erotic" I don't mean sexual, because you and I both know that eroticism has a sexual component.
But let's not fall into that trap by which sexuality gets opposed to
spirituality as if they had nothing to do with each other. We should
be able to talk about desire for God as erotic in a way that does not
sound creepy or profane. In fact, Christianity has a bold and vibrant
history of doing exactly that. The Christian tradition is loaded with
images that use bodies and bodily desire to communicate just how
fierce our desire for God can be.

From its inception, Christianity has drawn on the relationship
between a bride and her bridegroom as a metaphor to represent
communion with God. This notion of God as bridegroom did
not begin with Christianity; it existed in Judaism, and it appears
throughout Hebrew scripture. What Christianity did was suggest
that when we human beings come together in Christian community—aka the church—we become the bride. Paul fancied himself
a proud father who had promised his churches in marriage "to one
husband, to present you as a chaste virgin to Christ."[2]

This image isn't about Jesus and humanity sharing a metaphor-
ical cup of coffee while reading the morning news on matching
iPads. It isn't about humanity donning an apron, making a nice
home-cooked meal, and having it all ready on the dining room
table when God gets home from a long hard day of creating new
galaxies and waging war against cosmic evil. The ancients drew on
the metaphor of bride and bridegroom to point to something specific: sexual consummation. Paul expected his churches to remain
"chaste" until Jesus returned. The gnostic Gospel of Philip uses the
image of the bridal chamber to illustrate human redemption—our
reconciliation to God.

This is not an obscure motif in the tradition. That's what the
Song of Songs is trying to do: tell us about God by simultaneously
sexualizing spirituality and spiritualizing sexuality. Not denying either, but using both to convey something about the other.

Sex as metaphor for communion with God makes a lot of sense.
Imagine what it would really be like to encounter God. Not from

a distance, but up close. Such a spiritual union would have to be mind-blowingly intense. Could you put it into words? If so, what words would you use? What experience would you draw on for comparison? Would you talk about a really good meal? A gorgeous sunrise? Those can be amazing, sublime. But if you are talking about physically interacting with God, what human experience could possibly approach it except sexual union?

To compare union with God to sexual union does not necessarily mean that all sex approaches that level of the sacred—nor should "non-sacred" sex be demonized as profane. But if you are lucky, you know the extraordinary experience of coming hard in the arms of someone whom you love deeply, who loves you beyond measure. You know that this is a singular experience that differs in quality and intensity from anything else we humans do.

What the authors of these ancient sacred texts seemed to perceive is that the sexuality that comes closest to expressing divine communion is the sexual consummation that takes place in the bridal chamber, an experience that ideally includes and cultivates both spiritual and sexual connection. This is "marriage," not as so many people still want to define it, as a predominantly heterosexual union that is legal, exclusive, and privileged; but rather, as a spiritual relationship—a sacred relationship—that is expressed sexually as well as spiritually, physically, emotionally, economically, and so on.[3]

Many lesbians and gay men have long grasped this notion of marriage as a sacred/sexual union. Until very recently, our "marriages" were exclusively sacred/sexual covenants. That was what we had access to, it was what we intentionally invoked when we entered consciously into covenanted relationship.

We live in a time when it's common for people to reject mind-body dualism as antiquated.[4] Though it still influences Christian thought, I've never let myself get too hung up on dualism. Somehow I've always had a clear sense that these dualistic ideas were misguided, that a rigid attachment to dualistic thinking was a misinterpretation of an ancient idea, not intended to be applied to sexuality in a glib and condemnatory way. I have always sensed this, because I've always had the queer gift of knowing myself both as a carnal being and as a spiritual being.

Christianity sheds light on the queer relationship between carnality and spirituality by demanding that we grapple over and over again with the inherent, mindbending puzzle of God coming to earth as a human being. We Christians refer to this astonishing event as the incarnation.

The idea of God becoming incarnate is one of the richest veins in Christianity, offering vast opportunity to enter spiritually into an encounter with God. The stories of Jesus figuring out his own embodiment are pure gold, a gold that is seldom mined for even a fraction of what it is truly worth.

Many Gospel stories portray Jesus as being Mr. Compassion. You see this a lot in the healing narratives. Some leper gets up in Jesus's face to ask to be healed, and Jesus is filled with compassion and heals him.[5] The Greek word often translated as "compassion" is *splagchnizomai*. It literally means "a yearning in the bowels." Just try to pronounce it. It *sounds* like a yearning in the bowels.

Well, imagine if Jesus's compassion was like the word's literal meaning—a yearning that snuck up on him. In him, I mean. What if *splagchnizomai* was something that he didn't control or choose in some moment of remote divine objectivity? Maybe Jesus wasn't standing around all the time being pious and sounding Godlike: "Ah, here is a leper. I feel such compassion for this poor soul." Maybe his experience was a lot more like what happens when you're walking next to somebody who trips on the sidewalk, and even though you're late for work and you totally don't have time to stop, you just instinctively reach out to help right the person. And while you digest what just happened, somewhere deep inside, you get that yearning in the gut thing that makes you take an extra moment to look the person in the eye and ask, sincerely, "Are you okay?"

It is such a normal human instinct to reach out to someone next to you who needs a hand. If it really is a human instinct, then maybe that impulse isn't just a spiritual one. Maybe there is something carnal at work in it—something both carnal and spiritual.

And maybe what made Jesus such a provocative and compelling figure in his day was precisely the fact that he was so deeply in touch both with his body and with his spirit. Whatever dualism existed back then, whatever body/soul binary Jesus had to deal with, there is no question that he ruptured it. People watching him were astonished at the way his flesh and his soul worked together.

There is something very queer about this convergence of sensitivities, attunements, to the spiritual and to the carnal. That's why it should come as no surprise that so many queer people are fiercely carnal, at exactly the same time that we are highly attuned to transcendent beauty and joy. This is what makes it so clear that it is a lie to say there is no spark of the divine in us. This is what makes it so clear that we are not merely carnal, but incarnate: a potent mix of body and soul, of earthly and divine.

Incarnation is both a strength, creating opportunity for movement and expression, and a vulnerability. We know about both. And with a focus on our sexuality, we go public with the most vulnerable aspects of our incarnation, both physical and spiritual.

Of course, whenever you reach out from a place of both strength and vulnerability, you don't know what you are going to get back. The challenge in laying your soul or your body bare is that being touched in intimate places is sometimes exquisitely pleasurable, and sometimes monstrously painful. It is a paradox that to achieve the ecstasy of erotic connection, one must also risk—and all too often experience—agonizing pain. Sometimes you get both, ecstasy and agony, simultaneously.

Scripture tells us that this is exactly what it is like to be touched by God. This is one of those extraordinary lessons that Christianity inherited from Judaism. The word that communicates this potent, life-altering touch is Hebrew: *naga*.

One passage in which naga appears is Genesis 32: the story of Jacob wrestling the angel. Jacob, the grandson of Abraham, son of Isaac, is third in the line of patriarchs whose descendants will number as the stars in heaven, who will become the people of Israel. Jacob is fiercely alive, fiercely carnal. And oh, does he want. He wants to be firstborn; he wants to be blessed; he wants the stunningly beautiful Rachel. And he's not afraid to go after what he wants, even if it means he has to coerce his brother, or lie to his father, or work his butt off year after year for Rachel's father. Jacob is successful, and he doesn't need anyone but himself. Which means that he is also, in a sense, very alone. The encounter with the angel takes place after Jacob has gotten most everything he wants. He's rich, has two wives, a raft of children. He's set for life. Oh, except for one thing. He hasn't been home in a very long time. You see, a couple of those little schemes of his cheated and thus wildly infuriated his brother, Esau. Jacob has been on the run from Esau for his entire adult life. But now, as he grows old, Jacob wants something he cannot steal and he cannot earn: he wants to go home. To do that, he needs Esau to forgive him. And unbeknownst to Jacob, that brings God into the picture.

So Jacob sets off. Esau comes out to meet him. For all Jacob knows, Esau is going to kill him. The night before they are to meet, Jacob sends his family across the river, leaving him alone. This is the moment of reckoning. Jacob has to get right with Esau, but first, he has to get right with himself and with God. Some mysterious figure appears—a man? An angel? Whatever it is, this being jumps Jacob. They wrestle all night, neither of them prevailing. Finally, as dawn is about to break, the angel delivers a brutal blow to Jacob's hip—naga. This is the touch of God, and in this story, it may mean the death of Jacob. The next morning, Jacob limps to meet his brother. Jacob can't fight his way out of this one. His autonomy compromised, Jacob has to rely on Esau's love and forgiveness. Will Esau embrace Jacob, or kill him where he stands? They meet, and Esau throws his arms around his brother. At last, Jacob finds a kind of connection that demands reliance on another, one that demands vulnerability. At last, he is healed; he is home. That angel's excruciating touch, that moment of naga, has crippled Jacob for life; it has also saved him.

Naga also shows up in a famous passage from Isaiah.[6] Isaiah is standing inside God's sanctuary, mesmerized by the beauty and by the astonishing angelic creatures flying as they attend to the Most High. As smoke rises from the altar and fills the room, seraphs chant a rhythmic praise so stunning, so evocative, that for two thousand years, right up to this day, it has been sung every week as part of the Eucharistic feast in churches the world over:

Holy, holy, holy is the Lord of hosts;
the whole earth is full of [God's] glory!

Isaiah is both riveted and terrified by the spectacle. He cries out, "Woe is me! I am lost, for I am a man of unclean lips, and I live among a people of unclean lips; yet my eyes have seen the King, the Lord of hosts!" Suddenly a seraph flies up to Isaiah's face, carrying a hot coal from the altar. The seraph touches—naga—the coal to Isaiah's lips to blot out his guilt and free him up to speak. In that moment, God calls Isaiah to be a prophet. Just like the angel's touch in the Jacob story, this touch is one that both wounds Isaiah and saves him. Whatever pain he experiences from the coal searing his lips, he pushes past it. When God cries out, "Whom shall I send, and who will go for us?" Isaiah does not miss a beat. "Here am I; send me!"

Even more than Jacob, Isaiah comes face to face with this basic truth: God is terrifying. Angels are terrifying. Not because they are punitive (though they might be), but because true glory and majesty and love and strength are terrifying, chaotic, *big*. When this God touches you, you hardly know what to make of the experience. It is so intense, so extraordinary, as to be nearly unbearable.

We must seriously consider and understand both sides of the naga equation. The healing it brings does not mean that the wounds hurt any less; nor does the wounding cancel out the glorious freedom and joy that follow it. God's touch is exquisite; God's touch is excruciating. Comprehending love means honoring the truth of the paradox.

Knowledge of oneself, of love, demands to be proclaimed in a way that makes oneself vulnerable, that puts one in danger. Naga is the place where the paradox of risk becomes incarnate. Risk leads to a touch that wounds and heals, both, often simultaneously.

Queer people understand naga innately, not just as an individual experience of love, but also as a condition of identity, of life. For us, it is the price of membership, of belonging, of self-knowledge. Many queer people know that touching in this way involves terrible risk. We know that it will exact a price. And we do it anyway. We do it because it is also the most exciting, life-giving experience some of us have ever known. It is maddeningly thrilling. Exquisitely liberating. Scary as hell.

Queer experience points to the terror of love as love, not as punishment for rule breaking. It is common for Christians to approach Christian ethics as a series of rules, and to assume that God condemns us when we violate those rules. This is the same problematic misinterpretation we saw operating in the story of Abraham nearly sacrificing Isaac: God sets up rules and demands compliance with them. If we break the rules, this thinking goes, we are wrong and worthy of punishment. This is a flawed but powerful notion that has done immeasurable harm to queer people. Many of us are forced to confront again and again the internalized homophobia, biphobia, transphobia, and plain old sexphobia that this thinking breeds within us.

As a queer person matures in understanding hir identity, ze can begin to perceive that when we encounter punishment as a response to our identities, it is the punishment—not the identity—that is a problematic, inauthentic response.

There is strong scriptural support for this understanding. Perhaps the most vivid passage is in the First Letter of John, when the author meditates on what it means for us to declare that "God is love." The author writes: "There is no fear in love, but perfect love casts out fear; for fear has to do with punishment. . . . Those who say, 'I love God,' and hate their brothers or sisters are liars; for those who do not love a brother or sister whom they have seen, cannot love God whom they have not seen."[7]

So what does it mean to "fear God"? This is not a marginal phrase in the Bible. English translations of scripture spend a lot of time talking about "fearing God." It is easy to read these translations and jump to the conclusion that we are supposed to fear God because God has the power to hurt us. I mean, that's usually what fear is about, right? I fear things that might cause me pain. But maybe there is another way to think about fear.

Naga tells us that God's touch is a chaotic mixture of extraordinary blessing and extraordinary danger. Touching the sacred is risky—the opportunity to feel love like no other, and destruction like no other. It is thus exciting—and terrifying. Doesn't it make sense to be afraid?

How could one not be afraid of the risk, aware of the danger? Such awareness, such fear is what makes the risk of faith all the more valuable, all the more visibly courageous. But this is not the same thing as being afraid that God is filled with wrath, and that God continually directs wrath at us (us humans in general, us queers in particular). Perhaps when scripture advises us to "fear God," the idea is not that we are supposed to be cowering on the floor, whimpering for our lives. Perhaps it's just the opposite. "Fearing God" may be a matter of acknowledging the full truth of God's touch, and taking up the steep challenge to love fiercely, passionately, openly, courageously—despite all the risks that such love entails.

Often even the caring and compassionate side of love is no picnic. The author of First John does not suggest nonchalantly that this business of loving your brother or sister is easy, or self-evident. It can sometimes be very hard—wrenchingly hard—to love in an active way even the people you will always, no matter what, love deeply: your life partner, your children, your dearest friends, members of whatever community you need, the people you really rely upon.

This is where naga comes keenly into play. In those relationships where your heart is most invested, where you have power over someone else and where someone has power over you, this is where it matters to understand the complex relationship between love and pain. This is where it matters to understand the distinction between pain and punishment. This is where it matters to know who you are, to risk touching and being touched.

Queer people are not alone in living out these dynamics; everyone does. Indeed, this business of putting oneself intentionally in the path of love, of taking on its challenges and perils, laying one's soul bare to the agony and ecstasy of naga—this is what Christianity claims as its distinguishing characteristic. Christianity is at its heart a path, a posture: one that embraces our incarnate state while recognizing the vulnerability it creates, one that calls us to tend to each other when we are struggling, one that offers and demands in the name of God a conscious decision about how each of us will respond to violence and fear.

Queer people don't experience these dynamics occasionally. We are dropped into them daily as into a deep pool of water. We have to learn to swim in them, anticipate the shock, navigate the cold spots, luxuriate in our ability to float. Day in and day out we risk our lives in order to feel, to touch. We put the most vulnerable aspects of ourselves on the line. A great many of us learn to do this publicly, openly, in ways that other people can see and, we hope, we pray, respect.

An individual queer person may not see the sacred at work in this aspect of our experience. But as a priest, I see it clearly. It is the identity that exists within each of us and connects us to something bigger than ourselves. It is the call to proclaim that identity. It is the impulse to make that connection manifest, incarnate. I cannot but see God at work when queer people courageously speak our truth to a world torn by ambivalence, to people who fear the touch of another, of God, but who want it, who need it, fiercely.

On that score, queer people do the same thing that Jews have done for millennia, that Jesus did when he walked the earth, and that many of his followers have done since: we don't just feel the glorious sting of naga; we celebrate it. We strut down Fifth Avenue in New York, or whatever local community we happen to be living in, making our Pride, our fabulously incarnate selves, as visible as we can.

This queer heart, this queer body, with its persistent desires, fierce hungers, is scandalous to those who view God dualistically. God knows that. God knew that Ze would be viewed scandalously for embracing—entering—one of these bodies. And Ze did it anyway. *I love that in God.* I need that in God. I need to feel God taking my hand, bearing me up, because this path we are walking together is about to lead us directly into the heart of scandal.

CHAPTER 5

SCANDAL

Hope is a dangerous thing.

—MISS CLAUDETTE,
Orange Is the New Black

I'm a little jealous of you.

Yes, you, sitting there reading this book a year or more in the future from this moment when I am sitting here at my laptop, writing to you.

Yeah, I know you have challenges in your life. I know you struggle with relationships and money and all the usual stuff. I don't mean to say that my problems are bigger than yours, or that you have it easier than me.

It's just . . . you have this one thing right now that I don't have that I really, really want.

You have the ability to go onto Netflix and watch what for me, now, is the next season of *Orange Is the New Black*. I don't binge watch, but even pacing myself I can only make a new season last for a few weeks. Max. So I finished the most recent season a few months ago, and now I have to wait, wait, wait for my next *OITNB* fix.

The show is addictive. What hooks me is the way it gives multiple views of each character. Once you begin to develop some familiarity with an inmate, the show gives you that person's backstory. Who was she before she went to prison? How did she land there? The stories blow huge holes in whatever assumptions you might make about these women as convicts. Sure, some of them had been in one form of trouble or another for a long time. A few made one bad slip that cost them everything. Most of them tripped into the criminal justice system because they needed something: social acceptance, love, expensive surgery, justice for someone they cared about. Hope that you can get what you need and want is indeed a dangerous thing, as Miss Claudette says.[1]

I am not trying to romanticize these stories, or pull some liberal "oh, poor them" line. I know what it is to need, and so do you. I know what it is to do something questionable in order to meet a fierce need, and to live with regret about it for a long time. I bet you know about that, too. It's a difficult but inevitable part of being human. Revealing those needs, *OITNB* puts flesh and bones on characters who might otherwise remain superficial types.

And then there's all that girl-on-girl action. Part of the reason I love *OITNB* is that it gets so much right about lesbian relationships.

First off, of course, is that lesbian relationships are hot.

Second, lesbian relationships are hot. (What? It bears repeating!)

Third, lesbian relationships are intense. They are emotionally intense, and they have vast potential to be sexually intense. *OITNB* portrays all of this exquisitely, and then some.

My favorite show so far was in season 1: the colorfully named Thanksgiving episode that builds up to Alex and Piper reigniting their sexual connection. The match is struck at a party to celebrate a prisoner's upcoming release. Someone puts on some music, and the women start to dance. The sexual tension between Alex and Piper is already on rolling boil, and it's not a surprise when their dancing turns into an erotic display. The other women are totally into it and clear the floor to watch and clap.

Pennsatucky, the would-be Christian crusader, is not into it. She runs to Healy, the lesbophobic guard. Feigning offense—and blatantly lying—she draws down the power of the police state as if it were her own. Healy walks in just as Alex is grinding her ass into Piper's crotch. Healy is scandalized, oblivious to the jealousy that fuels his anger.

Healy accuses Piper of attempting to rape Alex and sends her to solitary confinement. Upon being released from solitary, she makes a beeline for Alex. Does this experience make her cower? Does she express remorse? Does she tell Alex that they have to cool down the electric current running between them? No, she does not. She pulls Alex into the chapel, where they claw off each other's clothes to make skin contact.

The chapel is where everyone goes to have sex. It's a delicious inversion of conventional piety: the sanctified space sexualized. In *OITNB* the chapel is the place where women go to feel alive, to taste freedom. Somewhat ironically, that makes the chapel *a place where people want to be.* As someone who has been a chaplain in an institutional setting, I can tell you: that's no small victory for what is all too often a cheesy, wannabe sacred space.

OITNB nails the essence of scandal, taking one conventional assumption about propriety after another and standing them on their heads. *The Oxford English Dictionary* defines "scandal" as "an action or event regarded as morally or legally wrong and causing general public outrage."[2] When you Google it, here are some of the synonyms that appear: outrageous wrongdoing, misconduct, immoral behavior, unethical behavior, shocking incident, offense, transgression, crime, sin.

This is why people sign up for text alerts and keep their pocketed phones on vibrate, waiting to see what shocking tidbit will appear next. People will go to great lengths to avoid finding themselves in the midst of scandal, and for good reason. Scandal usually exacts a price, sometimes a high price. But when it is someone else paying the price, it's hard to look away.

The word "scandal" comes from the Greek *skandalon.* In ancient usage, it means "trap," but it refers to a very specific part of a trap: it is the stick that holds the bait.[3] The word also refers to the unfortunate moment in which one takes the bait and falls into the trap and, as the contemporary definition suggests, to the reaction others have when they see you fall. Thus scandal is not just a trap, but an entrapment—the bait, the fall, and the punishment all rolled up into one spectacle hungrily consumed by a public bored with their conventional lives.

There are lots of reasons that scandal keeps people tuned in, but one of the biggest reasons is this: scandal is sexy. That is especially true when the scandal is about sex, which it often is. Temptation, succumbing to temptation, the gaze of others upon you as it plays out. . . . Lots of people—probably the majority of people—have navigated these dynamics at one point or another as they have navigated their sex lives. What queer people have always had to do is navigate them more publicly than others, for reasons we've already discussed. The relationships we seek are scandalous, still a moral outrage to many people and a legal transgression in many lands. This makes the ability to navigate scandal a matter of survival for us.

But we do more than survive in these waters. What Piper does as she dances with Alex is what queer people have done since the dawn of time. She sees the scandal brewing and steps right into the heart of it. Boldly. There is something on that turf that she needs, that she wants, and she marches in to claim it.

Queers are able to endure scandal, so many of us, because we have already confronted and survived the threats, the sanctions imposed by those who police scandal and punish its violation. We already know what it is to risk. We are well acquainted with the dangerous, wounding aspects of naga. Many of us perceive the stirring of an identity deep within, an identity that won't be denied and that cannot be written off by arbiters of social niceties as "scandalous." We as a people have long been able to find amusement in the notion that we are somehow shocking, scandalous. We laugh, snap, square our shoulders and proclaim with pride, "You need me to be a scandal for your little, impoverished worldview? Well, honey, so be it."

The facts of queer life demand a lived response of high moral caliber. Some queer friends gave me pushback on this idea. They feared that the words "high moral caliber" could be construed as an appeal to respectability, and they anticipated that many self-identified queers would resist such a call. I would resist such a call. The notion of respectability is itself a trap. It is a trap because our scandalous nature—and our courage in confronting convention—is at the heart of what we bring to larger society that is of such value. This is a paradox of huge ethical import.

Michael Warner's *The Trouble with Normal* is largely a call to resist efforts to become respectable members of society at the expense of our queerly scandalous/scandalously queer natures. He writes:

> In scenes where some mad drag queen is likely to find the one thing most embarrassing to everyone and scream it at the top of her lungs, in Radical Faeries gatherings and S/M

workshops—in these and other scenes of queer culture it may seem that life has been freed from any attempt at respectability and dignity. Everyone's a bottom, everyone's a slut, anyone who denies it is sure to meet justice at the hands of a bitter, shady queen, and if it's possible to be more exposed and abject then it's sure to be only a matter of time before someone gets there, probably on stage and with style.[4]

Warner is describing a gay male scene from the 1990s that is instantly recognizable to many of us who were in or near that world at that time. This scene doesn't exist today in the same way; nonetheless, the lessons he takes from it still teach us something important about what our lives mean. "In those circles where queerness has been most cultivated," he writes, "the ground rule is that one doesn't pretend to be *above* the indignity of sex. And although this usually isn't announced as an ethical vision, that's what it perversely is."[5]

The rules of queer culture constitute an ethical vision, Warner claims, because they establish social ties between and among us, social ties that make demands of us in terms of how we think about one another and how we treat one another. To be clear, Warner is not saying that we do not have intrinsic value as human beings. Rather, he is arguing for a self-awareness that is inherently relational. As Warner explains:

I call [this] an ethic not only because it is understood as a better kind of self-relation, but because it is the premise of the special kind of sociability that holds queer culture together. . . . The rule is: Get over yourself. Put a wig on before you judge. And the corollary is that *you stand to learn the most from the people you think are beneath you.*[6]

This is core Christian theology.

Queer people seem to get instinctively that transcendence, if it is to be desired, is best gotten by diving into embodiment: sex, design, beauty, service, *and* scandal, shame. It takes courage to be who we are in the face of rejection, spitting, coercion, threat.

Michael Warner and Piper Chapman both understand there is something of immense value that we seek—and to an extent find— in our performance of scandal. But don't let our ability to entertain and be entertained fool you. We know full well that scandal is dangerous. By definition, scandal offends conventional sensibilities. It upsets, disturbs. Scandal is unnerving because, according to conventional wisdom, *it's not the way things are supposed to be.*

This is one of the ways that Christianity is most thoroughly queer. Everything about Christianity is scandalous, from the inherent shock value of God becoming a defenseless baby, to the cosmic joke by which Rome's most shameful instrument of torture becomes a mechanism for salvation. The centerpiece of Christian worship is Holy Communion, where we share bread and wine that for some Christians represent Jesus's body and blood and that for Catholics actually become Jesus's body and blood. If the cannibalistic overtones don't make the case plainly enough that we are about scandal, try this on for size: the word "Communion" comes from the Greek word *koinonia*, which means "common." In Jesus's time, it also meant "defiled."

And that's the point. Scandal isn't an inconvenient by-product of the Christian tradition. The scandal of Christianity is completely intentional. The entire thrust of the Christian message is supposed to make our jaws drop, our eyes open as wide as they can go as we stammer, "But, but . . . *that's not the way things are supposed to be!*"

The Gospels communicate this in an interesting way. Instead of just saying over and over again, "Be shocked. Be very shocked," the Bible tells us stories in which people trip over this inherent scandalousness. We watch the protagonists of these stories struggle, and we listen to what Jesus says to them about it.

The most dramatic of these stories is an encounter between Peter and Jesus. Peter is a stock character actor in these little vignettes about how people struggle with what Jesus was up to. He specializes in roles that are designed to look clueless, shallow, or just plain dumb. The scene that Jesus and Peter have over the scandal of the cross is, really, just the worst for poor Peter. Jesus has just told the disciples that he is heading for Jerusalem where he is going to suffer and be killed. Peter wigs out. The text says that Peter pulls Jesus aside and begins to "rebuke" him. Can you imagine rebuking Jesus? Peter says, "God forbid it, Lord! This must never happen to you." Does Jesus place his hand compassionately on Peter's shoulder and help him process this difficult truth? No. Jesus is pissed. He assaults Peter with perhaps the most withering statement in the entire gospel: "Get behind me, Satan! You are a stumbling block to me; for you are setting your mind not on divine things but on human things."[7]

Peter is basically saying that he is scandalized by this idea that Jesus is going to suffer and be killed. Jesus responds by calling Peter a "stumbling block" to *him*. The Greek word is "skandalon."

In all of Christian scripture, this is the only time when the word "skandalon" is used to refer to an individual person. And here is something else. This little drama unfolds just two verses after the scene in which Jesus renames Peter, and in a famous wordplay, makes Peter the founder of his church on earth: "And I tell you, you are Peter, and on this rock [*petra*] I will build my church, and the gates of Hades will not prevail against it. I will give you the keys of the kingdom of heaven . . ."[8]

One minute Jesus is identifying Peter as the guy who is going to lead his movement on earth. The next minute Peter goes all establishment and begins reprimanding Jesus for the scandal of his fate. Jesus is astonished. "*You* are going to be scandalized by *me*?" Jesus understands how powerfully human society is drawn to safety, to respectability. He sees clearly that the church's need to be respectable, to be safe, will lead it inexorably to struggle with the scandal he is about to become. That's why Jesus calls Peter out on this again right after the Last Supper. "You will all become deserters because of me," he says, using the verb form of "skandalon."[9] Peter stamps his foot in furious protest, "Though all become deserters because of you, I will never desert you." But the sun has already set, and in just a few hours that cock is gonna crow . . .

This is a cautionary tale extraordinaire for those with religious authority, and mother church specifically: You are not above being scandalized by the very message you proclaim. Beware just how easily you can become a tool of Satan, a scandal to Jesus himself, even as you stand there jangling those keys to heaven.

The epicenter of Christian scandal is that cross. What happens to Jesus is so bad. People who are scandalized respond by shaming. So it wasn't enough to kill him. The political and religious leadership of occupied Palestine had to humiliate him, snuff out his life like a cigarette butt under your shoe on a filthy street. This is what scandalized people do. This is what scandalous people take on.

So they strung him up, in a hideously gruesome method of execution. Crucifixion wasn't just a terrible way to die. It was designed by Rome to be a public display of torture, a constant reminder to those people living in occupied lands not to mess with their imperial overlords. As a public display, it shone a bright, blinding spotlight of shame on its victims.

Everything about crucifixion is hard to watch—visually, physically, emotionally, politically, spiritually. You'd think that the early church would have looked away, emphasized something else about Jesus's death, or done what the contemporary church often does: work overtime to keep Good Friday solidly in the context of Easter, breezing past the crucifixion as an unfortunate necessity in order to get to the resurrection.

But there is a reason that the cross itself became the chief symbol of our faith. The early church couldn't stop looking at it, wondering about it, trying to make sense of it.

Paul, for one, focused intensely on the cross. He wrote about the cross even when he didn't need to, forcing it into people's faces. Why? Like any good Roman citizen of his day, Paul appreciated that death by crucifixion was designed to shame, to humiliate. And like any good Jew, Paul knew that the idea of God being shamed in this way was so horrifying as to be almost incomprehensible. All of which adds up to this: Pointing to that cross wasn't an accident, or an odd literary choice. He was telling his audiences, the people in his churches, that it was impossible to ignore the cross—and very specifically the scandal of the cross—and fully understand what Jesus was up to.

Paul unpacks this idea most clearly in a succinct paragraph from his first letter to the church in Corinth:

> For the message about the cross is foolishness to those who are perishing, but to us who are being saved it is the power of God. . . . For Jews demand signs and Greeks desire wisdom, but we proclaim Christ crucified, a stumbling block

[skandalon] to Jews and foolishness to Gentiles, but to those who are the called, both Jews and Greeks, Christ the power of God and the wisdom of God.[10]

In this passage Paul is dialoguing with two worlds of thought: Greek philosophy and Jewish theology. The gentiles of his day would have discussed the nature of reality in well-reasoned discourse as was characteristic of Greek philosophy. At the core of Jewish faith was the strong belief in the one powerful God, YHWH, whose salvific feats of creation and exodus testified to this God's existence and supremacy. Jews of his day would have looked for signs—acts of divine power—to authenticate anyone claiming to represent YHWH.

Both of these perspectives were part of the public airwaves in Corinth, where Paul had founded a small but solid community. The people in this church couldn't help but try to see their newfound faith through these two lenses, Greek and Jewish, but neither lens explained—nor, really, made any sense of—this radical message that Paul was trying to get them to understand. Because neither worldview could comprehend the essence of scandal that the cross simultaneously represented and ruptured.

In this passage, Paul uses the word *dunamis*, root of the English word "dynamic." Dunamis is the power of God that Jesus channels in order to heal people. By setting dunamis in opposition to skandalon, Paul is saying that something happens in this formula of identity, risk, touch, and confrontation of scandal—something that is so strong, so powerful, it blows the lid off of every puny conventional fear harbored in the human heart.

That's because this formula stands on its head everything that people conventionally think about what power is and how it operates. For Paul, this is a cosmic shattering of something that operates as a stranglehold on humanity: the idea that death is the most powerful thing we know. The scandal of the cross means that death and its affiliates—terror, torture, physical and spiritual agony—lose their potency as the ultimate stumbling block, the ultimate bait and trap, the ultimate outrage.

Paul sees clearly that this shattering opens up a horizon of ethical possibility, an ethical vision that in some ways parallels what

Michael Warner sees in queer experience: the ability to learn the most from those you think are beneath you.

The Christian message explicitly demands that folks with power—political power, religious power, economic power, any kind of power—pay close attention to the realities on the ground of people who don't have nearly as much power as they do: people who are hungry, poor, marginalized, sick; prisoners, refugees, widows, orphans. If you've spent any time at all reading the Bible, you know this list. It matters to take seriously that inside every one of those categories are real people, human beings who think and feel, who need to eat, who have sex, who hurt and love and laugh and struggle and just want someone to understand what they are going through—just like you. Most of us have found ourselves inside one or more of these categories. Whatever of those experiences you've had, you know: it doesn't help when someone assumes that your experience is an aberration, that what you are going through is simply "not the way things are supposed to be." It doesn't help because sometimes—not always, but all too often—when people equate "how things are supposed to be" with "good, right, just," they also equate "*not* the way things are supposed to be" with "bad, wrong, criminal."

That's often how people come to believe that struggling, or being different, is shameful.

Shame is a complex emotion that has to do with a sense that you are bad or that you've done something bad. It can be situational, and it can at times be valid: sometimes people are right to be ashamed of what they have done. You can also feel shame as a kind of deep embarrassment. Sexual shame is sometimes about this—a sense of awkwardness piled on top of intense vulnerability that you may not want exposed to the world, especially when you are trying to get basic needs met.

The threat of shaming gives scandal its power as an effective arbiter of human behavior. Shame is designed to keep us in line. But shame is not merely a tool. Wrestling with questions about our inherent worth is an unavoidable part of who we are. Warner argues that we need to hang on to shame for health, authenticity, and power. He would say that we ignore or deny our shame at our expense and at the expense of others.

He makes a valid point. Neither shame nor scandal are vacuous concepts. Shame, if it doesn't paralyze you, can breed a kind of humility. It is an ethical posture that makes it possible to "learn the most from the people you think are beneath you."

But as a priest I have also worked with many people for whom queer shame is a debilitating condition cruelly inflicted by sanctimonious devotees of various religions. Claiming to speak on behalf of God, these people of alleged faith work hard to convince beautiful queer souls that they are bad. Internalized, these messages of shame wreak spiritual havoc, not just upending lives, but all too often ending them.

This kind of shame is not ethically helpful. It makes it all the more difficult to see the stuff for which one really should be accountable.

The question that both queer ethics and authentic Christianity press is: What behavior is truly scandalous, truly shameful? There is a message here to the church: if you want scandal to be an effective arbiter of social behaviors, be very careful how you define it, what traps you set, and what bait you use.

If the concept of scandal has value, queer people are not the ones who are devaluing it. We have rejected its power because it has been used so often and so violently as a weapon against us. But there *are* traps that people fall into because they—the people—are wrong. Sometimes people take the bait and reveal that their true nature is corrupt. Queer people know a lot about this, too. We see it happen when someone who has been persecuting LGBTQ people is revealed to be a closeted queer, cheating on his wife (it's almost always a him, a powerful him). We watch the scandal engulf such a person, and we know that he is getting what he deserves. Not because he is gay, but because he is a hypocrite. And not just a hypocrite, but a malevolent one, so busy projecting his internalized self-hatred onto others that he cannot even see the people he is damaging.

The Christian concept of "salvation history" is the story of how God creates us, *declares us to be good* (that is, *not ashamed*), watches us periodically wander off, and calls us back. The episodes of "wandering" sometimes look like this: people engulfed in pain or fear come to believe that they are bad, shameful; and through this false belief, they bring those destructive qualities to life. Today, people very often do this by projecting their own sense of shame onto others, especially sexual shame. This is not to say that evil does not exist as its own power, but rather that it is possible to collude with evil simply by denying our inherent value—denying it in ourselves, or denying it in others. Honestly, what is "evil" other than a denial of everything God stands for? When it comes to us, what God clearly stands for, puts God's heart and incarnate body on the line for, is the idea that we are of infinite value to the God who made us in Hir image.

A person of faith has to perceive this truth in order to stop participating in the abuse of power, either as perpetrator or as victim. It's how any marginalized, abused community or individual throws off oppression, by declaring, "The scandal is not what you say it is. Yes, I was crucified. Yes, I am queer. Those things do not make me bereft of value as you say I am. I am who I am, empowered by God, and I will live with integrity."

This is the essence of LGBTQ pride. Queer theologian Patrick Cheng describes "healthy pride" as "the affirmation of one's intrinsic value and self-worth."[11] Pride is thus the antidote to debilitating shame. Pride makes it possible for a queer person to feel the healing power of dunamis, upending the death-dealing aspects of skandalon.

This is not always easy, and the LGBTQ community has not always gotten this right. To claim queer identity is to sail into the headwind of scandal—knowingly, deliberately. It is very hard to do so and to maintain a posture of integrity. As a community, we have struggled deeply with the competing impulses to hide our most scandalous qualities/members and to lift them up for the world to acknowledge. Those of us who take queer virtue seriously are forced to reflect on our past and come to terms with our complicity in the shaming of our own—butch/femme, drag queens, those who are trans* or intersex or bisexual. The strength of the LGBTQ movement, at our best, is precisely that we stand together, that we look directly into the scandal imposed by others and declare it null and void. We know that our truth is stronger than the scandal, and we know that experiencing that truth together gives us power to do extraordinary things.

When we do get it right, it is stunning. It captures the essence of what Christianity is trying to get us to do/be/understand. This inversion of human shame and scandal was at the very heart of what Jesus was doing on earth. By looking scandal in the eye, Queers and Christians rob scandal of its power to keep us down, and use scandal as an avenue to build us up—as individuals, but *through* community.

Christians and Queers share this common understanding: our ethical foundation lies in the communities into which we are received by grace, which we build consciously for ourselves and for others. It is our communities that give our risk meaning, that hold our touch, that shore us up in the face of scandal, that empower us to be the people we are called to be.

CHAPTER 6

ADOPTION

When I came into the bar in drag, kind of hunched over, they told me,
"Be proud of what you are," and then they adjusted my tie.

—LESLIE FEINBERG, *Stone Butch Blues*

Have you ever read a book that changed your understanding of yourself, of your place in the world? That's what Leslie Feinberg's *Stone Butch Blues* did for me. A fictional memoir of one butch's life from the late 1940s through the 1980s, the story rocks back and forth from brutal accounts of raids and bashings to extraordinary moments of courage and tenderness.

The book challenged me to look at my own prejudice. Coming out in the 1980s, I inherited an arrogant disdain for butch/femme culture. It was common then for white lesbians who were involved in the feminist movement to disparage what we perceived as an aping of the oppressive heterosexual gender roles that we sought to escape. Ours was a shame-filled response, the result of having been similarly disparaged by mainstream feminism in the 1970s. Feinberg's book put human faces on what to me had been merely labels.

I was surprised just how much of myself I saw in her characters, in their need of each other, in their determination to survive with as much integrity as they could muster. The world they inhabited was the one I would have inhabited if I'd been born twenty years earlier; the bars that were home for them would have been mine, too. Feinberg's book was a gift, a legacy. I read it and felt claimed by people I desperately wished to claim back.

In 1993 Feinberg held a reading at Judith's Room, a women's bookstore in the West Village. I had to go. I just wanted to be in the same room with her. After the reading, I had to stoke my courage to go up to her. I think I was trembling as I reached out to shake her hand. She looked me right in the eye, generously encouraging me. "Thank you for writing this book," I said. "I didn't . . . I didn't know . . ." I struggled to get the words out. "I didn't know that we were a people, with a history." She thanked me, and I turned to go. When I hit the sidewalk, tears spilled. I stood there for what seemed a long time, crying, shaking, caught up in an experience that I knew I would remember the rest of my life.

Leslie Feinberg gave me one of the most important gifts that one gets from community. It is the same gift that the butches in the bars taught her protagonist, Jess, as they lovingly straightened her tie: the knowledge of self that comes from belonging to others.

"We see you. We value you. You are a part of us."

These messages are bedrock for other messages that are crucial to a healthy conception of self: "Know who you are. Be who you are. Be proud of who you are."

Queer identity may be discerned in relative isolation, but it comes to life in community. That is where we find mentors and friends, teachers and fellow travelers, who help us discern how to live this life and what values to uphold. That is where our identities are not only validated, but celebrated. And in that potent mix, which has always felt to me like the very essence of love, one finds liberation. The LGBTQ communities to which I've belonged have inarguably improved my life, every one of them. The people I've found there have made and still make the risk and the danger bearable.

Because most queer people are not born to queer parents, we have to go looking for people who can help us understand who we are, who can teach us about our history. Our signature spaces have historically been bars and bookstores, places where we could find each other, relax, hook up, relate, and learn. Given our relationship to scandal, it makes sense that our earliest gathering spots were bars, places where people congregate under cover of darkness to imbibe beverages that are marginally illicit, supposedly off limits to children. Independent bookstores are also often provocative places where people gather to discuss literature, politics, science, art, and other essential dimensions of human experience. Like the salons that once were home to queer intellectuals, bars and bookstores have long been havens for us. We now have a robust network of community centers, political clubs and organizations, and even churches and synagogues—which is a good thing, especially for people for whom a bar is not a healthy place to be.

The point here is simply that we have always needed spaces to *exist*, places where we become visible to others. Forming community has always been a primary impulse for us. That may be true for all or most people, but it is particularly important for queer people who need to find one another in order to know ourselves as queer people.

"Adoption" is the word that signifies people who are not related by blood but who have claimed one another as family. Lots of people, not just queer people, use the word "family" to indicate a very close connection. But "family" has particular significance for queers: for a long time, it was a code word by which gay and lesbian people acknowledged each other as gay. "Don't worry, she's family," someone might have said to allay fears of exposure or homophobic abuse. Claiming familial connection is particularly powerful and important for people who cannot take for granted that their families of origin, their biological families, will embrace them.

Queer community is like that, for many of us. Globally, it includes millions of people. But it is also local, personal, intimate: a network of relationships between individual human beings who need each other, who care for each other, who are home for each other.

Maybe you have had an experience of that kind of connection grabbing your heart unexpectedly. It happened to me again just recently when I stumbled upon a paper written by my younger son. Leo is a smart, charismatic little guy whom my former partner and I were exceedingly fortunate to meet when he was just eight weeks old. He needed a home, and we scooped him up, laying claim to this gorgeous child with eyelashes to melt your heart. The adoption went through six months later.

The paper I found was in his school bag. I'm guessing it was part of his school's lead-up to Mother's Day. On the paper were sentence-starters like "I love my mom because . . ." and "The thing I most like to do with my mom is . . ." The final sentence began, "I know my mom loves me because . . ." In his eight-year-old scrawl, Leo had filled in, "I am her son."

Now, for most kids, that might be an obvious response: "Duh. I'm her son; of course she loves me." But for a kid who is adopted, there's no "duh" in the equation. To participate in an adoption is to become intimately aware of the fragility of human connection. If you have experience with adoption, you know: you learn not to take for granted the continuity of even the most primal attachments. Stories about adoption almost always involve hard realities—biological parents who made excruciating choices; various kinds of personal or familial brokenness, illness, death. Many kids who are adopted begin absorbing these truths at a young age. But with luck, those same kids also begin learning at an early age to choose, consciously, the families into which they have been received. Lots of adoptive parents can tell you some version of the story I just told, of that moment when they knew they had been chosen back, when they heard their child declare quietly but clearly, "I am yours; you are mine. We belong to each other."

The experience of familial brokenness is familiar to far too many queer people. I am one of the lucky ones blessed to have nearly unequivocal support from my family of origin. But even the fortunate few like me are only one or two degrees of separation from heartrending stories of familial rejection and violence. Our community has in recent years begun to pay deeper and much-needed attention to the plight of homeless and runaway youth. Our concern for these kids is personal. Studies estimate that as many as 40 percent of homeless and runaway youth are LGBTQ.[1] Many of them are children and very young adults who were thrown away by their parents or who ran away to escape emotional or physical violence. Many, many queer people either were one of those kids or know someone who was.

Queer people don't take for granted the idea that "family" is always healthy. Thus the metaphor of family helps qualify the caliber of those individual connections within our community. Like any family, we don't always get along. We don't always treat each other well. We don't always like each other. There are family members who are abusive; there are family members who refuse to acknowledge their familial ties; there are family members who enjoy tremendous privilege and keep it to themselves even as they watch others struggle mightily. And at the same time, there are family members who are extraordinarily generous. There are family members who pay attention to familial identity and call us all to account. There are family members who model graciousness and compassion and fierce love. We know what it is to be proud, in a good way, and we know what it is to feel ashamed for not living up to our own expectations of ourselves.

And as in a family, we know that it is important to keep the relative health of the entire family in view. This matters, because queer people can be abused by communities themselves. You can see this along intersectional lines: lesbians of color being rendered invisible or worse in communities dominated by white women; my own experience being casually dismissive of the life-or-death struggles of butch/femme culture; young people struggling to have their gifts and contributions recognized by older queers; battles between LGBTQ people whose ethnic or national allegiances conflict. Bisexuals are assailed for not being gay enough; trans* women and drag queens collide in an effort to name themselves and claim their respective turf; trans* rights disappear entirely from federal legislation designed to end employment discrimination against LGB— uh, let's just leave off the T, shall we?—people.[2] We sometimes disagree about the direction our movement should go. The title of this book—its use of the word "queer"—will be unsettling and even offensive to some people, especially to older people who once upon a time had that word spit at them in the midst of chronic, caustic assault.

These kinds of disputes can easily escalate to a point where an individual or group feels not just unwelcome, but oppressed by an entire community that exists under the mantle of LGBTQ. This happens. The pain is just as valid an experience of queer community as are experiences of empowerment, encouragement, and love.

So what can be said about LGBTQ community that is true? What can be said that Christians can appreciate?

We know our need of each other. Not all the time, or in every single circumstance, but overall. We need to have access to other queer people, to queer spaces, to queer thought. We need it for safety, but not just for safety. We also need it to know ourselves. We need it to know love. We need each other for basically the same reasons that people need family. And in the same way that people need family, we don't just need each other a little. We need each other deeply. We need each other to our core. Some people feel this need more strongly than others; but I don't think I've ever met anyone who was fully content to be an orphan.

For queer people, community is the crucible of our ethical lives. Precisely because we need each other so much, we set high standards for our behavior vis-à-vis ourselves and one another. Deliberation about the most pressing ethical issues that a queer person confronts is often informed not just by how the ethical decision affects that person or the people closest to that person, but also by how it affects the community and other queer people more broadly.

This is not a call to be aware of "how it reflects on us" when people behave a certain way. That impulse, that fear, is certainly alive in our communities, and you can hear it in our discourse. But many of us know that respectability is suspect, and our suspicion does sometimes win out over the temptation to join the ranks of those deemed socially respectable/acceptable. We have made real strides over the decades in recognizing the damage we have done to one another by trying to create a public impression that feels less threatening to the dominant culture. We have long been blessed by strong voices who call us back to remember that our ability to stir, confront, and survive scandal is one of our gifts.

When lived out with integrity, the ethical impulse of our communities is not a demand for respectability, but rather is a call to authenticity. That is why, bottom line, participation in community life is at the heart of LGBTQ experience. We need community; it needs us; it is us.

Participation in community life is also at the heart of Christian experience.

The Christian emphasis on community is a vital part of our Judaic heritage. Long before Israel was a modern nation, Israel was a *people* who possessed a visceral understanding of their identity as a family created by God, chosen by God, living in covenanted relationship with God. Jesus altered the basis for membership in that community but continued to emphasize its importance when, at the Last Supper, he blessed a sacred meal and identified its key components—bread and wine—as his body and blood. Today, "the Body of Christ" is an evocative phrase that refers both to the sacrament of Communion and just as importantly to the community of people—the global church—who are fed by it.

Jesus inaugurated what we now call Christian community. He had the vision, but the apostle Paul was the one who had to figure it out, explain it to people, and help it take root.

Paul, for all his faults, put his shoulder to that rock and pushed over the course of decades. Paul's workload was magnified by the fact that he was taking this message, rooted in Judaic thought, to people all over his known world. The brilliant Paul, a scholar of religious law, fluent in both Greek theology and Roman ideology, was a gifted translator, nimbly conversing in terms that both Jews and Gentiles—non-Jewish people living under the Roman Empire—could understand.

Early in his work, Paul was on fire. Paul's conversion on the road to Damascus was an amazing, vivid encounter that rocked his conceptual world.[3] As he rebuilt his worldview, he began to see certain truths with crystal clarity. They weren't theological abstractions to him. Paul had just seen these truths play out in the events surrounding Jesus's execution and resurrection. For Paul, these events were recent. They were real. They communicated a message that was urgent.

What was that message? This is a crucial, foundational question. In the conventional Christian narrative, Christianity is a radical rewriting of the covenant between God and Israel in which Christianity supplants Judaism as God's "light to the nations."[4] Progressive churches tend to wriggle uncomfortably with the unavoidable implication that Christianity is an improvement on Judaism designed to replace the original, a sort of Judaism 2.0. Many of us know instinctively that something is wrong with this conclusion. How do we proclaim a bold gospel that doesn't disparage our spiritual parent, the tradition of Judaism?

Brigitte Kahl, a German Protestant minister and biblical scholar, argues that Paul's message was much bigger, more radical, and much more practically important than a theological or even cosmological tug of war between two competing notions of Judaism.[5] Kahl states the obvious: the big player in Paul's world, the entity that was affecting absolutely everyone, was Rome. To justify its imperial domination, Rome promulgated an ideology of dualisms, of oppositional binaries, in which Rome was the great and powerful Subject/Self. According to that cosmic order, Rome was superior to and thus correct to impose its law upon less militarily powerful people, all those Object/Others, exacting all the tribute and deference that an occupied people customarily provide to their imperial overlords.

Key to that Roman mindset was the idea that Caesar was divine, which is why Rome considered it an act of sedition and not mere blasphemy when the earliest Christians declared that "Jesus is Lord." With this statement, early Christians denied not just Caesar's divinity but also the ideological justification for the empire. They announced that they were called to follow a God whose law is based on love and on raw courage, not on enmity and fear; a God who endured violence rather than perpetrated violence; a God who stood with them and called them to stand together rather than dividing them; a God who fed them rather than stealing the bread from their children's mouths.

The tension between Roman ideology and the message of Jesus as Christ was obvious to Paul and to people in every territory who were struggling under the weight of Roman occupation. It so permeated the air that it had to have been part and parcel of the message that Paul was delivering. Kahl argues that in all the letters where Paul talks about law as a force that enslaves, he is not talking about Jewish law; rather, he is pointing to Roman law, and to the binary-based, Self-versus-Other ideology that undergirds it.

Thus Paul perceived in the Christ event not a spiritual evolution (from Judaism to Christianity) but a cosmic battle in which Caesar manifested a lived ideology of fear and violence.

In this schema, Paul's mission had very little to do with reforming Judaism and everything to do with proclaiming the good news of Christ in order to break Rome's growing hold on the world. But he faced a challenge: Paul was bringing to non-Jewish people a message of liberation and hope that was founded solidly within Judaism. And the people of Israel were truly a people, a tribe, related to each other by blood, who had been called by God. How could non-Jews participate in this sacred relationship with the God that Paul and his people knew and worshiped?

Paul repeatedly uses the word "adoption" to refer to an individual believer's relationship to God. The first use is in his letter to the Galatians, immediately following one of the foundational rupturings in Christian scripture. He writes:

> There is no longer Jew or Greek, there is no longer slave or free, there is no longer male and female; for all of you are one in Christ Jesus. And if you belong to Christ, then you are Abraham's offspring, heirs according to the promise. . . . God sent [Hir] Son, born of a woman, born under the law, in order to redeem those who were under the law, so that we might receive adoption as children. And because you are children, God has sent the Spirit of [Hir] Son into our hearts, crying, "Abba! Father!" So you are no longer a slave but a child, and if a child then also an heir, through God.[6]

Paul's message astounded first-century people living under the boot of Rome: You are now free, he argued, a child beloved by God, who has claimed you as a parent claims a child. The God of Israel—who was also, to Paul, the God who anoints Jesus as Christ—this God does not want you to be enslaved, held captive, constantly afraid.

His reference to Abraham points to the identity of Israel as a people bound by kinship. As intimate as this language is, it is the language of community. Paul is explicitly transgressing boundaries that exist between tribes and nations, inviting people to enter into a new kind of relationship not just with God but also with one another. In this arrangement we are no longer Self-against-Other, but Self-with-Other: siblings in a family characterized not by internecine warfare, but by deep care.

It is one thing to say that Christianity is and must be queer. To read Paul is to understand that authentic Christian *church* is and must be queer. The church itself must be a place where binaries are examined and challenged. This is especially important when the binaries involve power dynamics or inform our ability to claim kinship with one another.

In exactly the same way that community is the crucible of queer ethical lives, community is the crucible of Christian ethics; and recognizing the inherent queerness to which our faith communities are called is crucial to understanding the ethical path that

Christianity sets before us in community, as a community. Just as in queer community, the call to Christians in community is not to respectability, but to authenticity.

How many churches today emphasize relationships of mutual respect and rigorous love even among their own congregants? Lots of churches encourage people to be nice to one another, and many, many churches provide extraordinary support to members of the congregation who are struggling. I honestly don't know how my younger brother and I would have survived my mother's death had members of our church not stepped up heroically to be present to us, and literally to house and care for us. That is all extremely important and right in line with Jesus's and Paul's teachings. But it is not the same thing as demanding an ethic of honesty, accountability, and hard love when a community is in turmoil or disagreement. It is not the same thing as expecting people truly to examine themselves and listen closely to oppositional others when there is dissension. It is not the same thing as resisting the impulse to create factions, to lobby behind other people's backs. It is not the same thing as demanding that people with decision-making authority make those decisions transparently rather than behind closed doors.

When did we lose the authentic message that Paul was proclaiming?

These changes took hold over time. Christianity changed in myriad ways when it became the imperial religion under Constantine early in the fourth century CE. The church stopped being a persecuted sect, which would have been a sea change for devout Christians. Inexcusably, collusion with Rome empowered many Christian leaders to become persecutors of others: Jews, pagans, and those deemed heretics. But the changes were not merely about status. The message itself changed. You see, Paul's message was working. Christianity *was* a threat to Rome, as it was and still is a threat to any coercive power when it is lived authentically. Once Christianity became the established religion of the empire, the church simply couldn't preach what it had been preaching. Paul's message began to be manipulated. The guiding ethical message of Christianity was badly warped at this point, and we never got it back. Kahl argues that "Paul more or less fell prey to a major 'identity theft,'" which now requires us to reexamine what Paul was trying to say about Self and Other, male and female, and law as a potentially coercive force. She concludes that centuries after Damascus, "Paul underwent a second 'conversion' in the Christian imagination, one that turned him posthumously into the mouthpiece of the very imperial order that had originally executed him as enemy and Other."[7]

What we lost is precisely the impulse to rupture dualistic, militaristic, oppressive binaries.[8] Before Constantine you have a church that is intentionally queering notions of self and other—both within the community and externally in the world they inhabited. After Constantine the church abandons the political side of this mission, and stops doing some of the most important internal work as well: the work of recognizing ourselves as members of an adopted family.

Christianity was never meant to be a religion that was handed down from one generation to the next, unself-consciously, like a piece of property. But today that's exactly how the church gets treated: like property. In some churches, the "property" is theological: doctrine that is set and rigidly maintained by people with ecclesiastical power. In some churches, "property" has a more literal meaning. The Episcopal Church, for example, was once the affiliation of choice for affluent people. Wealthy families poured money into grand buildings, gorgeous stained glass, exquisite linens and silver. Now, I am as enthralled by the "beauty of holiness" as anyone, and there are few things I love more than Eucharist celebrated in a breathtaking setting. The problem is that it gets too easy for people who have invested that kind of money into a church to feel that they own the joint and can dictate what takes place there. That's privilege at work, and it creates a dynamic that runs directly counter to the dynamic that we are supposed to be living as Christians.

Paul says that we are heirs, but Christianity is not an inheritance that yields monetary gain or any kind of social privilege. In fact, Christian inheritance moves in the opposite direction, calling people to give up their stuff rather than squirreling it away. Christianity is a relationship with God and with other people. It is the kind of relationship to which one commits oneself deliberately, determinedly: a chosen family.

That is what the church aspired to be in its early days, back when Paul was traveling all over the Mediterranean forming little communities of faith. He told a story about Jesus the Christ coming to earth, preaching, being targeted by Rome and Roman collaborators, and being executed by the imperial death machine familiar to every one of Paul's listeners. The idea that Jesus had come back from the dead—had beaten the crucifix that everyone so thoroughly loathed—would itself have seemed unbelievable, raising both eyebrows and hopes. That he did it without lifting a single weapon would have signaled to many that this was indeed God's hand at work. A God who would have done all of this would have caused jaws to drop in surprise.

But Paul didn't just try to tell people about Jesus, about God. Paul told people about themselves. When he baptized people, he echoed John the Baptist's cry for repentance, helping defeated people perceive the role that they unwittingly played in their own oppression. The call to repentance in baptism includes the radical insistence that people have power—specifically, the power to turn away from the death-dealing ideology of empire and to move together in a different, life-giving direction. Pile on top of that Jesus's basic posture of radical love and healing, and suddenly Paul was preaching a message that people were starved to hear. It was like the parable about the treasure hidden in a field.[9] For people who were touched by this message, it became the most important thing in their lives. One may dispute much of what passes for history in the Christian narrative, but there is no disputing this historical fact: people who met Paul suddenly were willing to put everything at risk, including their lives, in order to be part of the movement he was forming.

And so people came together, their hearts guiding them into a new identity, a horizontal identity. Were they choosing it, or had it chosen them? When your heart has been grasped in such a way, it can be very hard to differentiate choice from calling. And in some ways it doesn't matter. For us what matters is to notice that these people found themselves suddenly and dramatically on a path that is remarkably resonant with the path of queer virtue. They were caught up in a new identity, perceived from within, that was affecting all of their relationships, particularly their most intimate relationships. It demanded that they value themselves as children of God. It was an identity fraught with risk. Enormous courage was required to declare it—and not to deny it when the threat of persecution reared its ugly head. It was an identity that would have felt very much like being touched by God, a resurrection touch that would have smelled simultaneously of death and of rebirth, of wounding and of healing, of destruction and of salvation. It would have plunged every single person who experienced it deep into scandal. And it would also have brought people together, people who needed to live this new life in community.

The experience of the early church would also have been like LGBTQ experience in this way: people in the early church knew their need of each other. They needed each other so they would not be alone in this amazing experience. They needed to meet, worship, and share meals. They needed each other for some measure of safety, but not just for safety. They needed each other to know love. They needed each other to have some kind of home, some kind of family. And in the same way that people need family, they didn't need each other a little. They needed each other deeply. They needed each other to their core.

Very importantly, they needed to know what this new identity would demand of them, what obligations it was going to impose. We have explored what it means to enter into a community that is fundamentally queer, charged with renouncing false binaries, characterized by horizontal identity: a community in which people know their deep need of God and of one another. What are the ethical obligations that such a community takes on? How might an appreciation for queerness help progressive Christianity understand itself and its mission? This is the question to which we now turn.

PART II

A PRIESTLY PEOPLE

*A priest is someone who stands in a place of
remarkable vulnerability, and by doing so,
invites other people to enter the sacred.*

This definition of priesthood, offered to me years ago by a friend
who was entering the ordination process, is the best definition of
priesthood I have ever heard.

In many Protestant traditions we talk about the "priesthood
of all believers." We assert that all Christians should view themselves as a kind of priest, whether they are ordained to holy orders
or not. This means, if you take my friend's definition seriously,
that those who call themselves Christian must know what it is to
stand in a place of vulnerability in order to invite others to enter
the sacred.

One way a priest does this is by living a relationship with the
sacred in a way that others can see. That's why a priest's vulnerability is important—people can see it, and be encouraged by it,
and join into it, knowing that they aren't alone in approaching
the sacred. A priest thus consciously cultivates an awareness of
the sacred, and conspicuously lives in a way that makes entering the sacred more possible. A priest lives into the realities that
theologians perceive. Which is to say, a priest connects the lived
reality of our lives with a theological understanding of the God
we worship.

The title "A Priestly People" is a double entendre. It suggests
that queer people en masse have a priestly quality—a quality that
Christianity ignores, or worse, disparages to Christianity's considerable impoverishment. In this section, we will explore several
ethical locations where queer identity places concrete demands
on individuals and on the community—where the rubber hits the
road, so to speak. Any person who has had more than a casual

acquaintance with queer community has most likely encountered these ethical issues. They are central to queer sensibility: the understanding that the most important thing we can do for ourselves and for one another is to tell the truth—about our inherent value; about who we are; about the multiplicity of our experiences; about who is still struggling and what they/we are still struggling with, and what we are going to do about it.

But the title has a second meaning as well: it is a way to understand a call to authentic Christian life. There are many people of good heart who not only call themselves Christian but who also take seriously the queer/Christian ethics that we've been discussing throughout this book. Some of those people—some of you—are already familiar with the idea of "the priesthood of all believers." Some of us are even comfortable walking around in that identity, claiming it for ourselves, daunting as that may at first seem.

An appreciation for queerness can revitalize progressive iterations of Christian life and thought by *making us better priests*. Not just those of us who have been ordained, but all of us who call ourselves Christian.

Making oneself vulnerable, consciously—as a queer person must, as a priest must—requires that one know oneself. It demands risk. It involves touching others. There is something scandalous about it. And it is foundational to our ability to be in community with each other.

CHAPTER 7

PRIDE

P ride begins first and foremost with the ability to see oneself. Self-perception can be challenging for any human being. If you carry inside of you an identity or an experience that is disparaged or shamed by others, the challenge is magnified. Many people, not just queer people, know a lot about these dynamics. But not seeing your true self creates a problem. If being seen by others is a prerequisite for a relationship of trust, being able to see yourself is certainly a prerequisite for self-trust, which is fundamental to a consciously chosen ethical life.

New York Times columnist Charles M. Blow writes about the importance of self-perception in the essay "Up from Pain," in which he names his experience of surviving childhood sexual assault and explores with nuance his awareness of his bisexuality:

> Daring to step into oneself is the bravest, strangest, most
> natural, most terrifying thing a person can do, because
> when you cease to wrap yourself in artifice you are naked,
> and when you are naked you are vulnerable. But vulnerabil-
> ity is the leading edge of truth. Being willing to sacrifice a
> false life is the only way to live a true one.[1]

Taking this step helps Blow begin at last to come to terms with his childhood trauma, and it opens a window of possibility for a freer life. Having begun to acknowledge the truth of his identity and desire, Blow rapidly begins to carve out the parameters of his own value:

> I had to stop romanticizing the man I might have been
> and be the man that I was, not by neatly fitting into other

people's definitions of masculinity or constructs of sexuality, but by being uniquely me—made in the image of God,
nurtured by the bosom of nature, and forged in the fire
of life.

Shedding all of the "other people's definitions" with their pro-
jections onto our bodies and souls, letting go of the "man I might
have been" in order to "be the man" I am, a queer person searches
inside himself in order to declare:
I exist.
This is not a minor declaration of the patently obvious. There
are entire theologies dedicated to the idea that we do not exist as a
people. The whole "love the sinner; hate the sin" trope is based on
the premise that queerness is about what you do, and that it flies in
the face of who you actually are. That's why it matters to conceive
of queerness as an identity marker: it is essential that we refuse
to capitulate to queerphobic attempts to treat our relational lives
and our sexual encounters as something separate from our deepest
knowledge of ourselves.
I exist; I am queer; my queer self exists.
Very often the catalyst for that moment of self-understanding—
I exist—is the perception of someone else's queerness. This is why
our visibility as a people is so vitally important. These two aware-
nesses sometimes cascade upon each other so rapidly—*I am not
alone; I exist*—that it can be hard to determine which one comes
first. They may, in fact, be two iterations of a single thought.
John Cameron Mitchell and Stephen Trask explore these dynamics in their extraordinary musical *Hedwig and the Angry Inch*. A
punk rock meditation upon the ideas of love and sexuality, selfhood
and relationship posed by Aristophanes in Plato's *Symposium*, the
show features Hedwig, the "internationally ignored song stylist"
whose male to female sex-change surgery goes horribly awry. The
surgery allows Hedwig to marry an American GI and escape com-
munist East Berlin, but it deposits her in a territory of sexual identity that is unrecognizable, thus unnerving to many of the people
she encounters.
From the moment the show opens, Hedwig's existence is thrust

defiantly in our faces. Hedwig's man, Yitzhak, introduces us to Hedwig by equating her with the Berlin Wall, running down the middle of a split city, despised yet weirdly clarifying. Quoting Paul, Yitzhak identifies Hedwig as a dividing line between East and West, between slave and free, between male and female. Standing like a wall between these binaries, Hedwig calls attention to our impulse to enter and demarcate the spaces on either side of her. People become attached to these demarcated spaces, identifying with them. Losing the divide, however loathed it may be, is confusing. It pisses people off.

But Hedwig is quick to note that a wall bears an uncanny resemblance to a bridge, illuminating not just the demarcation but also the connections between the two sides. In Yitzhak's list of binaries, Hedwig occupies both sides, but neither fully. This both/neither location is the essence of the bridge and the wall that she is for us.

What I love about the image of the bridge is that it shows what is constructive in the rupturing that queer people do in our daily lives, both for ourselves and for others. We confront binaries to which people are deeply attached, to which they look in order to understand themselves. Sometimes this is liberating; sometimes it is confusing. This poses an interesting question to each of us as witnesses of such queering: what is it exactly that we want to tear down, the wall that divides, or the bridge that by its very existence offers—and perhaps demands—new ways to understand ourselves?

Both Hedwig and Charles Blow trace the crucial movement from "I exist" to "I have value." This dawning awareness is the movement into what queer theologian Patrick Cheng calls "healthy pride."[2]

Healthy Pride is an inversion of one of the conventional notions of pride. Colloquially the word "pride" can refer to an excessive level of self-esteem that keeps people from engaging other people. It can also refer to a determined, isolating self-sufficiency: someone can be "too proud" to receive assistance from someone else.[3]

But queer Pride isn't like that. Queer Pride demands and depends upon relationship—which is to say, an individual's Pride is bolstered by immersion in community. It involves a reciprocal dynamic in which one's sense of self-worth feeds and is fed by relationships with others.

Hedwig totally gets this. Her journey is largely toward a self-conception in which she knows that, although she stands in a divide, she is whole unto herself. Being "whole" doesn't erase her wounds, but it doesn't keep her isolated, either. She does not suddenly become an utterly self-sufficient person who doesn't need others. By the end of the show, Hedwig's ability to see herself as a complete human being leads her to invoke a community of other provocative musicians like herself and stand to join them.

Hedwig then sings a mantra that becomes nearly a mystical chant, calling us to lift up our hands. The audience in the show hardly needs to be told twice to get our hands up. The song is called "Midnight Radio," a reference of deep significance to the power of music in Hedwig's life. Hedwig encourages each of us to understand ourselves as transmissions of infinite worth, and to share that understanding with one another, transmitting, receiving, our hands raised in the air to amplify the connection between us.

Evangelicals will recognize this gesture as one in which a person lost in the ecstasy of communal worship instinctively lifts up her hands to invite the sacred into her body and soul. Lifting up one's hands can be a way to connect to something bigger than oneself, something that might even be transcendent. Whether Hedwig intentionally invokes the religious aspect of the gesture or intentionally subverts it, it is no surprise that a show so thoroughly queer would grab people's hearts (and, yes, our souls) with such power. In that moment, the audience members become the people to whom Hedwig is singing: me, you, all of us acknowledging our brokenness, each of us called to know ourselves, know our self-worth, and help each other to know it, too.

Pride is exactly like that. Pride is a statement of personal affirmation that extends out to others. Pride calls us together. In this way, Pride becomes a posture that makes ethical living possible. In fact, it makes ethical living not only important, but often riveting, substantive, worth the price of admission.

Reaching deep inside the individual soul/psyche, reaching out to connect us to each other, Pride is very like what Paul describes in 1 Corinthians 13 when he writes about love as the glue that binds a community together. That's what Pride does for LGBTQ community. It binds us to one another. And true to Paul's description, Pride is very like—and may in fact be—love enacted.

PROGRESSIVE CHRISTIANITY AND HEALTHY PRIDE

If you were to try to sum up in a single word the difficulty of being both queer and Christian, the word "pride" would pretty much do it.

There may be no concept more sacred to queers than "Pride." But look in Christian scripture and hymnody, and you'll see "pride" condemned as a glaring and destructive human sin. Disparagement of pride is rampant in Christianity, and don't for a moment think that queer people fail to make this connection. When the word "pride" shows up in Christian liturgy, it is usually synonymous with hubris. Conventionally, pride can refer to the valuing of the self over and against the other. When defined this way, pride is a manifestation of a deeply imbalanced relationship between Self and Other. Calling people to account for harboring this kind of pride is one of the ways that Christianity pays attention to this imbalance, which in a way is a good thing. Aggressive, hubristic self-aggrandizement absolutely can and does come at God's expense, resulting in a stubborn refusal to participate in God's vision for humanity or even to recognize God's transcendent power.

But we need to be careful with our language. Defined like this, "pride" becomes the exact opposite of queer Pride. The two concepts are not only definitionally opposed, but also energetically opposed. Hubristic pride is the antithesis of healthy relationship. That's why in Christian theology pride is in no small way the essence of sin: hubristic pride makes relationship with Self, Other, and God nearly impossible.

By contrast, queer Pride is all about a healthy relationship with Self, Other, and for many of us, transcendent reality. Awareness and celebration of Pride thus involves a complex understanding of Self, of Self-in-Community, of Self-and-Community, and of Community itself. The complexity of these dynamics makes many of us queers keenly aware that our Pride is born of something deep within that connects us to one another, and also to something bigger than all of us. For some of us that "bigger than all of us" points to God; for some of us it points to big-picture truth and meaning that is authentic if not divine; for a great many of us it suggests and at times demands moral decisions, speech, and activism.

Progressive Christianity is often lacking in this kind of self-understanding. One seldom hears progressive Christians talk about Christian identity at all. Many, perhaps most progressive Christians consider their faith to be an affiliation rather than an identity.[4]

An affiliation is not a bad thing. Since it often focuses on one's relationship to a community ("I belong to such and such church . . ."), it may have some good Christian stuff going on. But an affiliation doesn't get you very far down the path to a healthy kind of Pride, because it doesn't necessarily contain the layers of connection that exist inside identity. Identity involves something going on deep inside of you—a knowledge of yourself. That deep self-knowledge is connected to something going on inside of a bunch of other people—a knowledge of ourselves. Our corporate self-knowledge is connected to something going on inside the community as a whole—a knowledge that was given to us by the One who created us. The sum of all of that self-knowledge is what propels us out into the streets to proclaim the truth of our identity, build a better world, and open those doorways to the sacred.

Looking to queer experience might help progressive Christians perceive both an identity in our faith and a way to feel a healthy kind of Pride in that identity. If we are going to ask queer people for help with this, however, we need to establish safe space in which we can work together.

In times like these when people are sensitive to the ways that words can do harm, it makes sense to lift up Christian disparagement of pride and ask churches to cut it out. We have no business asking queer people for whom Pride is a life-and-soul-saving concept to stand in a church and disparage the term. It would be useful if Christians could begin dismantling and rebuilding liturgical components such as prayers and hymns and replace the word "pride" with language that more accurately characterizes the problematic posture or behavior.

This is right in line with other language choices we make all the time. But it is not enough. It would be a big mistake to approach our relationship to Pride as a matter of mere political correctness, something that can be rectified with the tools of linguistic switch-eroo. Something important is going on—and being communicated —in the respective relationships that the LGBTQ community and the church have with the word "Pride"/"pride." We are better off digging into these dynamics and seeing what work, what promise, is here for us.

For more than half a century feminist and other liberation theologians have confronted the problem of equating sin with self-aggrandizement. Valerie Saiving launched this important movement in 1960 with the publication of her essay "The Human Situation: A Feminine View,"[5] now considered a foundational text in feminist theology. Judith Plaskow, a Jewish theologian, followed with the book *Sex, Sin, and Grace* in 1975.[6] The premise of these works is that any definition of sin that discourages people from asserting their own value and needs does vast harm to people whose value and needs are already being actively denied. Defining sin as pride, as hubris, may be appropriate for people of privilege—and especially for those who hoard power or who profit by appropriating resources from others. But for those who have been colonized, dehumanized, demonized, and in myriad ways robbed of life and livelihood, this definition works to extend and exacerbate their oppression.

Imposing such a definition of sin on human beings is one of the biggest hammers in the ideological toolbox of empire that Christianity was born to dismantle. This is ironic, because you'd think that defining pride as aggression and hubris would serve to contain imperialistic tendencies. I mean, that's what theologians would say is the whole point of defining pride in this way. But in practice, universalizing this definition of pride is one way the privileged Self absorbs and renders invisible all those less-privileged Others. Demonizing Pride is, in fact, one of the most effective ways that Christianity has ended up serving those who conquer and dominate, contributing to the disempowerment of people the world over.

Once you begin to see the ways that nominal Christianity has been warped to *maintain* rather than *rupture* violently oppressive binaries, it is also possible to see how easily the weaving unravels when one simply tugs on the bright threads of a consciously queer

Christianity. One of the brightest of those threads just begging to be pulled is the one we call "Pride." The fact that Pride is now lived out so colorfully, so vibrantly, so visibly by queer people all over the world makes it a thread that is fairly easy to locate and grab hold of.

It is a legitimate question to ask if this notion of Pride actually squares with the Christian tradition. Where in the tradition can we actually see someone claiming a healthy, balanced kind of Pride?

Some of the most prominent figures in Hebrew scripture begin their work by giving voice to healthy Pride. They are people whom God calls by name. When they hear their names, these people sit bolt upright and respond with the Hebrew word *hineni!* which means, "Here I am!"

God calls out, "Abraham!" And Abraham says, "*Hineni.* Here I am."[7]

God calls out from the burning bush, "Moses! Moses!" And Moses says, "*Hineni.* Here I am."[8]

God calls out to the child Samuel, serving in Eli's temple, "Samuel! Samuel!" And Samuel jumps up with a child's energy, ready for anything: "*Hineni!* Here I am!"[9]

Hineni is a vital concept in Jewish theology. It is the prophetic response to God's call—a call that is issued to individual, vulnerable human beings. When God calls people by name, big things are about to happen. Abraham is about to prove his faith in God's promise. Moses is about to liberate the Hebrew people from slavery. Samuel is about to restore integrity to the priesthood and, eventually, anoint David to be King of Israel.

The person who says "hineni" is basically saying two simple things:

Yes, it's me, the one you are calling;

I'm right here.

Hineni is thus a statement of identity and presence. That's why hineni is a declaration of healthy Pride. The person names hirself, declares hirself to be present. And all of that happens well before the person has a clear sense of what ze is supposed to do. As we try to walk this path of queerly Christian virtue, our first step is simply to cultivate an awareness of ourselves, while declaring ourselves present to God. We are essentially giving God someone to work with.

Hineni is the response of one who is wide open, poised for action. The prophet never has any idea what is about to happen, but he stands ready. And it's worth noting that the prophet isn't standing there, hands on hips, imagining himself to be some kind of superhero. After the prophet's brave response, God usually explains the task: "Moses, my people are suffering. I'm sending you to Pharaoh to bring them out of Egypt." At which point the prophet does a total double take and begins to backpedal like crazy. "Wait . . . what? You want *me* to go to Pharaoh? I think you meant to call my brother, Aaron, the charismatic one who can talk. Really, you can't possibly want me for this job."

God always just rolls Hir eyes and insists, "I called *you*, Moses. By name. *You*. Not Aaron. *You*. I'll be right there with you. We are going to do this. Together."

Moses' reticence may be familiar terrain for you. Perhaps you know what it is to enter into a project, or take a new job, and after plowing enthusiastically into some morass, you find yourself asking, "Holy crap, what have I gotten myself into?"

You need to know up front that the ability to tolerate discomfort is a requisite component of Pride. Healthy Pride can feel awesome, but it is not about entering a "feel good" zone and nesting there. Pride acknowledges fear so great that it threatens to paralyze even a guy like Moses. Pride demands courage. When God shows up and calls you by name, you may be slogging through some very hard stuff. Abraham declares, "Here I am," in the midst of the story of God demanding that he sacrifice Isaac. The aural backdrop to Moses's assertion, "Hineni," is the anguished groaning of the enslaved Hebrew people. Samuel is just a kid who initially thinks he is being called by his mentor Eli; but the message that God hands him is one that "will make both ears of anyone who hears it tingle," and when God says "tingle," Ze does not mean "with delight."

Hineni isn't prominent in Christian theology, but one of the few instances where someone gets the assignment, processes it, and *then* says, "Here I am," is in the Gospel of Luke. It's the story of Mary being visited by the angel. Gabriel appears and tells her she will be impregnated by God with a child who will be holy, who will be called "Son of God." Mary remains remarkably composed through this entire ordeal. Angels are notoriously terrifying, but Mary merely tilts her head with cautious curiosity. She listens, and ponders, and when the angel asks what she thinks, she tells him. This is a foundational story in the Christian tradition, and not just because it is the story of how Jesus is conceived. The fact that the angel talks with Mary, calls her by name, and waits for her to decide whether or not she wants to be part of this little experiment in divine/human comingling is revolutionary. Women just didn't expect to be treated with such respect back then. Thus the encounter foreshadows Jesus's high regard for women, which was radical in its day. It also signals a shift from other *hineni* stories: the one being called by name responds not with fear but with conviction and hope. While the process Mary is about to undergo may be terrifying—and the social stigma truly awful—there is also immense joy embedded in the outcome of her pregnancy, which Mary seems immediately to perceive.

Mary takes in all of this complexity, and she rises to the challenge. Her response is calm, self-possessed, measured, deliberate. The NRSV translates it as, "Here am I, the servant of the Lord; let it be with me according to your word." The King James Version translates it as, "Behold the handmaid of the Lord . . ."[10] Both translations point toward Mary's strong sense of herself. She stands in her Pride, knowing herself, able to meet this angel in conversation and engage her God in whatever extraordinary encounter is about to take place.

Pride should help you to stand with confidence. It's important, therefore, to consider what Pride means to you. Remember that we are talking about a healthy kind of Pride. We are talking about Pride that points to something deep inside you, something that is of immense value, something that connects you to other people and to God. As Christians, our fundamental identity—the thing we are supposed to know to our core—is that we belong to God. God created us, and we are dependent on God for our very existence. Very importantly, our tradition teaches us that God created us for the sheer joy of it, out of love. Take a few moments to ponder that. Then take a few moments to ponder the word "Pride" in that context. One of the images that comes immediately to me is how proud

I am of my children. That's one of the healthiest kinds of Pride I know, rooted so strongly and so obviously in the joy and love I feel for my kids. I'm not proud of them only when they accomplish something amazing; even when I am so mad that there is smoke coming out of my ears, I am crazy about those boys and proud of them beyond belief. Take a few moments to ponder what it means, what it feels like, for God to feel that way about you.

Pride in that sense is rooted in a commitment to believing that you are truly valuable. This is neither simple nor easy. Cultivating a sense of your own worth can be hard work. Queerfolk will tell you: for us, rooting out all the internalized homophobia/biphobia/transphobia/queerphobia is a lifelong endeavor.

And honestly, Christians have a trickier path here than queers do. Cultivating Pride is tricky for Christians because we must embrace our value as children of God while simultaneously rejecting all the triumphalist, militaristic, hubristic crap that still pervades our tradition. If you grew up singing "Onward, Christian Soldiers" practically every other week in church, you know how hard this is. We have to be queering those imperialistic interpretations and tendencies, constantly. If we are going to "Lift High the Cross," we need to be very clear: it's not an act of conquest, nor a proclamation of superiority to others. You and I both know that's just not what Jesus was about. Lifting up the cross is a way to say that we aren't afraid of love. Standing there, knowing the violence that gets directed at love, we affirm the Christian premise that though our bodies may be killed, our souls cannot die.

Ditching all holier-than-thou inclinations and trappings is only one of the challenges Christians face in claiming our Pride. Here's another: healthy Pride should not be hidden under the bushel of faux meekness and humility. The cross has an "in-your-face" quality to it, which we Christians are supposed to own. The inherent scandal of the cross is a huge part of its power. The cross should provoke people to question our attachment to—our investment in—the power of death. Our challenge, therefore, is to cultivate a kind of Pride that is akin to what Hedwig eventually internalizes for herself: Pride that is based on a deep appreciation for the divide in which we stand. Like those who dance into the streets to join queer Pride parades, we join those who are scandalous in a gutsy procession designed to tell people that we aren't afraid to be implicated in the scandal that God's love essentially is.

This is a narrow road, and it is challenging to walk. But it is no harder than the immense challenges faced by the prophets. Hineni is the response of someone who is about to stand up and look an extremely difficult situation in the eye. Pride is the self-awareness that gives you the strength to do that. And honestly, the key is that Pride takes your entire life seriously, all of it: the good and the hard, the joyful and the agonizing. Pride is able to be fully present to your toughest loss. Pride resides even in the places where you have been most badly hurt. Pride gets you through not by denying that the hurt is real, but by validating the pain and helping you to survive it. And Pride brings you into authentic relationship with other people precisely by equipping you to do the same thing for someone else: validating another person's pain, and standing strong with that person as ze faces it.

Healthy Pride makes it possible to feel good about yourself in a way that empowers you to treat other people better. It is entirely possible to cultivate a kind of self-love that makes you more compassionate, more sensitive to the lives and experiences of people around you. It is entirely possible to feel your own strength in a way that helps you be part of the solution when your community is trying to figure out how to navigate a difficult situation and move forward into a healthier place. It is entirely possible to be Proud in a way that encourages (en-courages) you to be vulnerable, and invites others to be vulnerable—and Proud—too.

If we are to use queerness to help us understand our own identities and Pride, Christians must become aware of and resist the impulse, conscious or subconscious, to deny the existence of LGBTQ people. Nominal Christianity is a principal enforcer of heteronormativity in the world today, and that enforcement is very often literal, used to justify the most severe punishments meted out to queer people all over the world—whether by vigilante perpetrators of hate crimes or by agents of state-sanctioned hate. This is one of the most virulent and visible ways that Christianity is currently being warped to maintain rather than rupture insidious binaries.

It matters that progressive Christians reject attempts to use Christianity to justify hateful teachings and violence. I hope that's obvious. But our Christian call demands something deeper of us. Our attempts to proclaim a more authentic Gospel will not go far enough unless and until we become conscious of heteronormative impulses within our tradition and work to dismantle them. These impulses are on glaring display in what often passes for Christian sexual ethics; so if you want to observe and discuss how our tradition views heterosexual relationships as normative, sexual ethics is the easiest place to start. Responding to the advance of marriage equality, some denominations are now engaged in conversation about what marriage signifies, and what makes a marriage "Christian."[11] If you belong to one of these denominations, perhaps this is a conversation you can join. Sexual ethics and marriage are not the only places where heteronormativity is plainly visible in our tradition, but if you are just wading into this stuff for the first time, they aren't bad places to dive in and get your bearings.

If you are going to do this, you need to know going in that it will at times be unsettling work. It may also feel profoundly liberating. Regardless of how it feels, it will demand a lot of you. You will need to develop an ear for the queerness in our tradition. That may challenge you, and if you come out of the closet with whatever you hear, I can guarantee it will challenge people with whom you converse. That's why Lisa Isherwood and Marcella Althaus-Reid assert that "queering theology requires courage."[12] They write, "In the same way that people sometimes need to renounce a beloved who has ill-treated them, we face here the challenge of renouncing beloved sexual ideologies, systems of belief that even if built upon injustice have become dear to us, especially if associated with the will of God." This work, they write, is not different from theological work to liberate our tradition from "former ideological abusive loves, such as racism, sexism, indifference towards the poor (if not active collusion in their oppression) and colonialism."[13] It's hard work, but so worthwhile, because what we are talking about is bringing our tradition into authentic dialogue with the truth of people's real lives, and real souls.

We queers exist, and many of us have lives and sensibilities that don't fit neatly into heteronormative constructs. And honestly, that's a good thing. Our perceptions of our relationships and ethical obligations are at times of a different hue from the perceptions informed by heteronormative Christian ethics. Far from an ethical deficit, that difference is often shot through with valuable insight.

Pride doesn't come easy. It requires courage. It demands honesty and self-assessment that is at times quite rigorous. You see, Pride isn't just a feeling. As something that is connected to your identity, it also draws you out. It makes demands of you. The good news is that you can practice it. You can start with small steps, practicing and building the courage that Pride requires. One of the most important steps is the one you take when you come out to others.

CHAPTER 8

COMING OUT

Queer experience often begins with some level of awareness, the flickering discernment of an identity. Coming out is the process by which a queer person gets honest about it. This part of the process entails risk and requires courage. Coming out, first to oneself and then to others, is a matter of personal integrity. It requires a measure of safety and an ability to trust—to trust oneself, at the very least.

The phrase "coming out" is tied to the concept of "the closet." The closet is the place where one can stay cloaked, metaphorically; where one's sexual identity is not seen by others. Lesbians, gay men, and bisexual people have had to grapple with what we call the privilege of the closet: that our sexual identity is often, though not always, something that one can choose to hide or to disclose. This makes sexual identity different from skin color (though not always), or sex (though not always), or using a wheelchair as your primary mode of getting around.

Decades ago people who identified as gay began to realize that the single factor that most affected how someone felt about "homosexuality" was whether that person knew someone who was openly gay.[1] The more clearly we came to understand this dynamic, the more we understood that coming out is not just a personal statement. Coming out is an act that changes the world. Coming out makes it easier for the person standing behind you in the closet to come out—and the person behind hir, and the person behind him, and so on. Once you really grasp this, it is hard to ignore the corollary: not coming out makes it that much more difficult for the person behind you to come out as well. A friend of mine, almost twenty years older than I, recently said, "Not coming out is never a morally neutral act."

The reason that coming out is so important is that it is crucial to building community, and community is crucial to building a measure of safety. But community now exists, and that means that for many people coming out does not need to be the solitary and often perilous act that it once was. This is not to say that it is no longer dangerous. The violence against our people is still menacingly alive. We face emotional violence and physical violence at the hands of family members, fellow students, bullies on social media, preachers in the pulpit, mobs on the street, and, in many parts of the world, cops and courts and judges within the legal system.

But it is also true that people are safer, overall, in places where LGBTQ communities are strong. Coming out builds up the community, and the existence of that community provides support, encouragement, and balm to those who come out. As a community we have visibility and political power that allows us to organize against the violence directed at us. Thus there is reciprocity between an individual and the community, a dynamic tension between the imperative to come out and the solid ground one needs to take the risk—the solid ground of relationships with people who know you, who see you, who love you, who understand what you face, who share some aspect of this part of you and who love it in you and in themselves.

For LGBTQ people who are not yet out in significant arenas of their lives, there may be an inherent paradox in the tension between the need to create community and the need to have community in order to be safe. The simple truth is that lots of us have come out in relative isolation. Many of us still have to do this. You may well be the first person in your school to declare that you are trans*— even if you live in a large metropolitan area. You may be the only person you know in your faith community who is intersex. You may live in a town where a young lesbian just had the shit kicked out of her on a public sidewalk, and suddenly whatever small group of queer people you know about has gone quiet. You may feel alone, and even the knowledge that others have gone before you and faced in other places what you face now may not feel very comforting— not when you are the one about to take the risk.

If you are not yet out, know this: queer people all over the world take you and your life very, very seriously. Figuring out how best to keep you safe is a vital conversation among many people in places where community exists. The need to be yourself, to be true to your essential dignity, is part of that formula of what it means to be alive and whole and safe. This is what Charles Blow is talking about. You are not alone in trying to steer that course, trying to figure out how much courage should be demanded of you. That's another crucial part of LGBTQ community: we need each other to navigate these complex ethical issues.

We are called to perceive an identity within and to proclaim it even in the face of risk. But we don't need to do that with reckless disregard for our well-being. If you are struggling to come out, in any part of your life, make a safety plan for yourself. This can be as intense and rigorous, or as easy and fluid, as the situation you anticipate facing. But seriously: think and pray and plan. We don't need more martyrs. We need strong, loving people to witness to the truth within us. We need you, and we need you to be alive and whole.

With your vulnerability in view, marshal whatever support you have. Identify both friends and other sources of support in your area. Is there an LGBT community center near you? Is there a Gay-Straight Alliance in your school? Reach out to these people. Is there any chance that you are going to need a safe place to go after you have whatever conversation you are planning? Think about where that place is, and talk in advance with whomever will let you in and be with you there. It's good to know there are people around who care; it's even better to get their active help and support. If you don't yet have anyone that you personally know and trust, you can call the New York City Anti-Violence Project (AVP) hotline to talk through your safety plan.[2]

Are you likely to encounter spiritual violence from someone when you come out? Unfortunately, the answer to that question for most if not all of us is "yes." I strenuously urge you to create a spiritual safety plan for yourself, *whether you consider yourself to be a spiritual person or not.*

All queer people face spiritual violence. Not coming out won't protect you from that violence. All you have to do is read a news story about marriage equality, or employment nondiscrimination, or efforts to organize a local Pride parade—anything that involves lifting up the value of LGBTQ people. You are very likely to hear someone saying terrible things about queer people. It won't matter how "diplomatic" people try to be, or how much they deny that they are being bigoted. And it won't matter if you have given up on faith altogether, or if you are an atheist, or if you have vowed never to step foot in a church/synagogue/mosque/temple ever again. Your soul knows when it is being disrespected or, worse, assaulted. It hurts. Spiritual violence is nasty, insidious. It does real damage.

Find someone who can affirm the beautiful queer soul you are. Find a good friend who can speak that language with you. Find a faith community that will affirm you. If there isn't an affirming faith community or minister in your area, go online and find some of the myriad cyber-communities (blogs, news sources, etc.) that exist to affirm queer lives. You are not alone. And you are not alone in having to confront spiritual violence. Other people need you to be their community, their support, too. Find each other. Take care of each other.

Given that so many of us face violence when we come out, how do any of us balance our personal need for safety with the community's need for us to emerge and be visible? This is a complex question that demands a lot of soul searching and a lot of courage on the part of individual queer people. What is clear is that many of us keenly feel our obligations to each other—both as truth tellers and as those who must work to keep each other as safe as we reasonably can be.

If you are someone who is observing rather than living queer virtue, do not fail to appreciate the rigor with which LGBTQ people approach these kinds of ethical questions. Sometimes you hear people use phrases like "moral relativism" to describe ethics among those who support justice for LGBTQ people. Because we have thrown off the moral absolutes that unequivocally condemn queer sexual behavior, the thinking goes, we have no real ethical grounding. Those who make these claims say that there isn't anything we truly believe; our ethics blow with the prevailing wind.

This simply is not true. Queer people do not categorically reject absolute truth. We do view the concept of "absolute truth" warily, and we tend to take great care in our claims about truth. This caution is not a symptom of moral relativism, but is born of our awareness that callous, ill-informed appeals to "absolute truth" have caused vast suffering. It *is* true that we don't usually get very deep into moral reasoning before someone asks, "How does this principle affect people's real lives? Whose story does this take into account, or ignore?" We don't do that because our *morals* are constantly in flux; we do it because we recognize that *people's lives* are. Indeed, the impulse to take people's real lives seriously is itself a moral absolute for many LGBTQ people. This impulse is an essential, characteristic strength of our ethical thinking.

COMING OUT AS CHRISTIAN: HEALTHY EVANGELISM

"You are witnesses of these things."

According to the Gospel of Luke, this is one of the last things that Jesus says to his disciples before he ascends to heaven.[3] With this statement, Jesus gently but firmly encourages the disciples to understand another aspect of their identity. They are not merely creatures of God; they have now become witnesses to the power of God—and specifically, to the power of God to overcome the violence of the Empire. This is an identity that carries a particular obligation: to go out and tell people what they have witnessed.

When the disciples own this new identity and take seriously its obligation, the word "witness" becomes a verb. Christians talk about the importance of witnessing to our faith. But how do we do this? There is arguably not a single aspect of Christianity that so completely eludes progressive church members. And because Christians aren't demonstrating a healthy, respectful way to evangelize—literally, to "tell the good news"—the folks who suck up all the air are the people who too often turn evangelism into something small and offensive.

Little wonder that the progressive Christian footprint in the collective cultural consciousness is so faint. We seem barely able to talk about our faith; we hardly know what to say. When asked about the most basic concepts in our religion—flesh, spirit, sin, forgiveness, redemption—many of us fall silent, or begin to stammer half-formed thoughts. Those of us on the Christian Left can be quick to criticize the Christian Right when it promotes pat answers to life's challenges, but we also often fail to draw on the strengths of our tradition to grapple with the hardest truths of life in a rigorous way.

If evangelism is hard or even confounding for you, take a moment to absorb the core messages of faith that we have been discussing. Ponder a God who loves you like crazy, who wants to be loved back by you, who values your love, who values you. Ponder this God who also loves the people around you like crazy, in all our diversity. Ponder this God who is amazed by our efforts to find Hir, who smiles at the myriad ways that we enter mystical space to experience and celebrate the sacred. Ponder a God who gets so sick at heart of all the violence we stupidly perpetrate, who is so disgusted by all the justifications people come up with for hurting each other, that every few millennia this God actually steps into human history to do something about it. Ponder a God who is willing to be hurt by Hir own creation if it will remind us who we are supposed to be.

Understand that we are not talking about an action-figure God who shows up on the silver screen surrounded by dazzling computer-generated special effects. Can you picture in your mind's eye a God who is real, who accomplishes the unimaginable feat of undermining abuses of power without actually abusing power Hirself? Can you imagine the One who would rather see you healed than punished; the same God that you maybe pray to for help, for guidance; the One whom you hope will show up when you are hurt and lonely and in desperate need of some love; the One who perhaps has done this for you at some memorable point in your life?

How badly do you want to be caught up in a movement that understands God in this way? How fierce is your desire to enter into sacred reality—especially if it looks and feels like *that*?

Remember that this God has created you to be in community with other people who yearn for the same life you do. Imagine what it would be like to be reminded, every time you are in the same place, just how real and powerful and exciting and terrifying and important your life together is. If you can imagine that, you are already well down the road to comprehending a healthy kind of Pride.

Can such a dream truly live within a Christian church? Queer theologian Elizabeth Stuart argues that it can. She stands her ground with other queer members of the church, recognizing that the tradition is not finished or static, but is constantly evolving:

> We believe, against all the odds and outward appearances, that [Christianity] can be redeemed from oppressiveness, because from the beginning it has had some inbuilt resistance to what has been made of it and there have always been Christians even in the darkest of days who have picked up on this liberating strand.[4]

You can be one of those Christians, picking up on that liberating strand.

Maybe you are already doing that. Maybe you live it; maybe you have found it in a vibrant, friendly church that treats kids well and has a nice cluster of gay people in regular attendance. That's great, truly. But understand this: our faith tells us that it isn't enough to believe it quietly, to go to church on Sunday with less fanfare than you might go to brunch, or to the grocery store. You have to explain to people what you are doing, and why it matters to you. What you are feeling, perceiving, and perhaps living out in community with others is caught up in what Jesus called "the good news," and it matters very much that you tell other people about it.

The most important thing that progressive Christians can do to advance an accurate understanding of our faith is to *come out as Christian*. And specifically, to come out *as the kind of Christian you truly are.*

The task here varies depending on what people know or are likely to assume about your faith. If you aren't talking to people in your life about your spiritual path at all, then you will need first and foremost to open that conversation. If you live in a place where people already assume you and most everyone else in your town are Christian, or if the people with whom you interact on a daily basis already know that you belong to a church, then clarifying the content of that faith is perhaps more important than simply stating it.

The necessity of coming out is one of those basic things that progressive Christians should be learning from queer people. When you know who you are and what you are about, it matters to tell people about it. But listen up, all you shy Christians out there: queer people know something that you may not know. *We know how to do that.*

Begin by getting in touch with your own identity, with Pride. Coming out is first and foremost a conversation that is about *you*. This matters to understand: you aren't coming out to people in order to change *them*. Hopefully you are coming out because your life matters to you, and this other person matters to you, and you want that other person to know who you really are.

Coming out is a very personal process. You are choosing to make visible a part of yourself that you value deeply. Precisely because you care about it, it is a part of you that is vulnerable. You have to go into this process knowing that you are taking a risk. When it is scary or confusing or disorienting, try to remember the theology of risk that we talked about in chapter 3: "risk" is the verb form of "faith," and it is shot through with love.

Queer people will tell you: you are the authority on your own process. You will know whom you need to engage, and you will have the best sense of how to do this productively.

To whom should you come out?

Consider coming out to anyone who is important to you. This includes people whom you love, who love you, who by virtue of your relationship should know important things about you. Using queer experience as a guide is helpful here: if this is someone whom you would tell about a new romantic relationship, maybe that's someone to come out to as a Christian.

Sometimes queer people come out for practical reasons. Maybe you aren't especially close to your office mate, but your social relationship is such that you'd have to obscure details of your life in order to hide the fact that you go to church. That feels gross, so you find a way to come out. If you live in a place where people assume that you are a conservative Christian, you may need to address your discomfort with the way a coworker casually ropes you into conversations that assume conservative Christian norms.

Start with the easy people: people who love you, who will want to understand something that is important to you, who will want your relationship to become deeper as a result of your honesty and the respect you are showing this person.

What will you say?

Summon your inner prophet, and your inner priest. Your inner prophet says, "*Hineni*—here I am." Your inner priest stands there in vulnerability, opening lines of communication. Your prophet cares mightily about telling the truth; your priest tells it in a loving and respectful way. You want to make this easy for people to understand. The whole point is to be yourself, and to invite conversation.

Don't think for a moment that you need to have figured out a rigorous theological argument about what you believe. If you want this conversation to go well, lead with your heart and keep it simple.

If saying "I'm a Christian" is too hard, maybe you could start with, "You know I go to church. It's really important to me. And I want you to know that. I want us to be able to talk about it."

If you don't belong to a church, perhaps you can start with something like, "I've been looking for a church to go to. I haven't found it yet, but . . . something important is leading me to look. You really matter to me, and I want to be able to talk with you as I figure out what this is all about for me."

If you need to clarify the kind of Christian that you are, can you identify something that is personally at stake for you? Do you worry about your daughters growing up listening to conservative Christian talk about submission? Remember that you aren't trying to start an argument. You are trying to witness something that is going on in your heart—to own it, and to invite the other person to observe it with you.

I can easily imagine you sitting there thinking, "Um, Liz, don't I need at least a little theological content? The preconceptions out there about what it means to be Christian are pretty big. I think I'm going to need to respond to that specifically."

Excellent point.

To have that deeper, more thoughtful conversation about the content of your faith, call on your inner prophet. A lot of people think that a prophet is a person who tells the future. In fact, in the Judeo-Christian tradition a prophet is simply one who tells the unvarnished truth. Of course, you and I both know that there is seldom anything simple about telling the truth, and that varnish goes a long way toward making difficult truths easier for folks to sit with.

Walter Brueggemann notes that prophets tend to be most

visible "in subcommunities that stand in tension with the dominant community in any political economy."[5] It's not a stretch, I think, to observe queer people as just such a subcommunity. But pause for a second and consider the subcommunity not just of queer people, but of queer Christians and Christian allies of queer people. What would it mean for us to observe progressive, queer-positive Christianity as a "subcommunity" standing in tension with the "dominant" community of queerphobic, nominal Christianity?

From the church's earliest days as a sect in the Roman Empire, Christianity has called its members to stand apart from trends in the dominant culture that are deemed spiritually problematic or sinful. This is what it means when people talk about Christianity as being countercultural. For example, many Christians both on the right and on the left often feel we are being countercultural when we stand in opposition to consumerism and conspicuous consumption. In today's multicultural world, with a growing awareness of intersectional dynamics, being countercultural is a complicated matter.[6] Sadly, it is now common for people to think that what Christianity is supposed to stand counter to is a certain iteration of contemporary social mores. In September 2014 the *New York Times* ran an article that began, "Religious institutions often see themselves as countercultural—outposts in an increasingly secular society that challenge the culture with views and practices that are no longer mainstream. But inevitably, culture seeps in, affecting how clergy and laypeople dress and pray and behave toward one another."[7] The article is about a study that finds that American congregations are "increasingly open to gay men and lesbians." The reporter is using the term "countercultural" as shorthand to refer to, among other things, some churches' reluctance to embrace LGBTQ people. This is an unfortunate misconception about what "countercultural" means for Christianity.

Progressive Christians today are increasingly aware that secular society is correct to move away from suffocating sexual constraints. We know that something is deeply wrong with church teachings that cling to misogynist and queerphobic theologies. It is a source of embarrassment to many of us to have to admit that, in fact, the secular world is increasingly getting it right while the loudest voices in Christendom continue to get it wrong. This phenomenon all by itself goes a long way toward explaining what is so hard about coming out as a Christian.

Viewing ourselves as countercultural within our own tradition may offer a way out of this trap. Understanding ourselves as countercultural against the dominant strains of queerphobic and triumphalist "Christian" teachings gives us a new way to conceive of ourselves. And importantly, it gives us a way to describe who we are when we are trying to explain our identities as Christians—like when we are coming out to others.

Now, it matters that we not ignore whatever privilege exists within our churches and denominations. We as a movement are not being persecuted and oppressed by megachurch pastors and their small town evangelical kin. Or I should say, we progressive church types aren't being collectively oppressed. We queerfolk most certainly are. Globally. That's why it's so easy to comprehend queer Christians as prophetic witnesses in the way that Brueggemann describes.

That's also why this work, this business of coming out, is so pressing.

The simple truth is, progressive Christians have the option to recognize ourselves as a subcommunity in tension with dominant Christian culture—and we have the option not to do this. We can join forces with queer Christians who are being beaten up by dominant Christianity, sometimes in our very midst, or we can choose to stay quiet. In queer parlance, we call this "the privilege of the closet," a term that describes the parts of our identities that need to be disclosed in order to be perceived by others, as opposed to those that are immediately apparent to others.

When you have the option to stay in the closet, you may be tempted not to stand in solidarity with people who don't have that option. And lots of us progressive Christians are so closeted that we've furnished and decorated our cozy little nooks and installed air conditioning to keep things from *ever* heating up in there. But closeted Christians need to recognize that there are people who are being thrown under the bus, crushed by hateful proclamations of a false gospel, while we rest in the comfort of our tiny personal sanctuaries. We can see this in history when, for instance, so many white churches hemmed and hawed on violent practices such as slavery in the United States, or took decades to stand up to the racial terrorism of lynching. Queer people have for years been visibly harmed by the ambivalent proclamation of progressive Christianity, but queer people are not and never have been the only ones to suffer while the left wing of the church waffles for the sake of false peace.

People, it is high time for every one of us to end our complicity in this spiritual violence by coming out.

Brueggemann says that our job boils down to this: "Prophetic preaching is an effort to imagine the world as though YHWH, the creator of heaven and earth, the Father of our Lord Jesus Christ whom we Christians name as Father, Son, and Spirit, is a real character and decisive agent in the world."[8]

Ultimately, that's what you are doing when you come out. You are declaring your faith in—your deep hope for—such a God. There is nothing small about this. In truth, it is not just the tradition of Christianity that is often misrepresented as colluding with oppression. God Hirself is misrepresented. God does not "hate fags," as some earnest churchgoers have asserted. The passages that abound in scripture urging us to show generous hospitality to the strangers among us, to the immigrant, to the Other, these passages communicate powerfully not just who God expects us to be but also who our God is.

Declaring your faith in this God is precisely how you witness to the truth that Jesus is Lord and not Caesar—that is, that God is a God of love and not of coercive violence. Your trust in God so defined is its own energetic refusal to bow down to violence, and proclaiming your trust in such a God is one of the most important ways you can actively *resist* forces of violent control and *invest* in the powers of love and faith, fueling their capacity to shape our world.

This is how you witness to the courage that Christianity demands. Christians sometimes obsess over the rules that we think we are supposed to follow. To elevate obedience above courage as a virtue is simply not authentic to Christianity. Mere obedience seldom helps us to address the persistent and challenging issues regarding Self and Other that surround us. We live in a world that is complex, and we are called to tell the truth about that complexity,

CHAPTER 9

AUTHENTICITY

If the foundational statement of Pride is "I exist," then the foundational statement of Pride in queer community is "We exist." For the community to be whole and authentic, we have to peer into this statement deeply, and literally. We exist as people with complex lives, with intersecting and hybrid identities. Queering as a discipline demands an appreciation for nuance, for complexity. Queerness in community demands that we respect the nuance and complexity of one another's authentic lives. Fortunately, we as a people have a knack for this. Recognizing the ways that we queer the binary of male and female probably makes it easier for us to comprehend that other kinds of people are also queerly intersectional and hybrid in their identities. Because we are born into families that span every race, religion, nation, and socioeconomic status, our community is inherently diverse. The art of queering therefore both obliges and facilitates our ability to declare that "we exist" in all our complexity.

It is challenging but essential work to become aware of how our various power-infused particularities (things like race, religion, skin color, sex, gender identity, ability, immigration status, access to wealth) interact and consciously or subconsciously reinforce one another. "Intersectionality" describes this complex web of privilege and oppression. "Hybridity" describes the impact of colonization on racial identity, and the impact of hybrid racial identity on power dynamics and cultural expression. Queerness demands that we take these dynamics into account in our ethical lives.

Awareness of and respect for intersectionality and hybridity are among the most important ethical calls of our movement. Not just because we tend to be sensitive to these dynamics, but also and more importantly because they have everything to do with power. People who are seen and recognized have vastly more power than people who are rendered invisible.

Justice for queer people is increasingly a global movement. In this our work aligns with other efforts that will ultimately require global action, such as movements to address environmental degradation, religious persecution, human trafficking, and extreme poverty. Traction on any of these issues will require an understanding of local social and political dynamics along with an ability to communicate and coordinate across lines of language, culture, and tradition. This means that we need to hear, understand, and respect each other. Awareness of intersectionality and hybridity—respect for the truth of our lives—affords opportunities for better dialogue, more effective strategizing, and the cultivation of honest solidarity.

Failure to recognize intersectional and hybrid identities is more than a missed opportunity. Very often willful ignorance of these dynamics is at the root of the problem at hand. It is an old tactic that has long been used with maddening effectiveness by those who persecute queer people. For example, in the wake the Right Reverend Gene Robinson's consecration as the first openly gay bishop in the Anglican Communion, it was common to hear political and religious authority figures across the world intentionally muddying political discourse regarding laws that criminalize queer identity and behavior in their countries. These leaders assailed homosexuality as an intrusion of western decadence, and accused those who protest these laws of colonial hegemony. Mahathir Mohamad, former prime minister of Malaysia, offered the standard version of this argument when he "reiterated claims that foreign powers were trying to dominate weak countries and warned that Western influences threatened Malaysia's traditional values."[1] Mahathir was quoted as saying, "Western films idolize sex, violence, murders, and wars. Now they permit homosexual practices and accept religious leaders with openly gay lifestyles." This bit of propagandist jujitsu was particularly ironic given that Malaysia's law criminalizing homosexuality is one of the Section 377 laws first introduced under British imperial rule in the nineteenth century—that is, it is the law, and not the protest, that is the result of colonial meddling.

The point here is not to charge anyone with behaving hypo-

critically—however accurate that charge may be—but to emphasize how hard these laws' proponents work to render invisible the
people who are being most harmed: LGBTQ people living in these
countries.

Patrick Cheng gestures toward what is so problematic in this
kind of dehumanizing maneuver, and he names it as sin:

> Society perpetuates the myth that all people of color
> are straight (and thus are opposed to LGBT issues), and
> that all queer people are white (and thus are opposed to
> issues relating to people of color). This is particularly true
> when society wants these two groups to be pitted against
> each other, as has been the case with the marriage equality
> movement. This, of course, renders queer people of color
> as nonexistent.[2]

Cheng is writing about race and sexuality, but he could also be
writing about sexuality and national or ethnic identity. Defenders
of the Nigerian and Ugandan laws criminalizing same-sex sexual
activity, for instance, seem to imply that there is no such thing as
an African person—especially an African person of color—who is
born queer.[3]

Queer people take these dynamics very seriously within our
communities because they are tactics that have been used so effectively against us. We know well that invisibility robs us of both
dignity and the power to combat our own oppression. Recognizing
intersectional and hybrid identity is not always something we get
right, and we have at times been slow on the uptake. But overall
LGBTQ communities do as well or better than any community of
which I've been a part in recognizing these dynamics and working
to perceive and make visible multiple layers of human identity and
experience.

Claiming our existence, our identities, and our power are all
necessary if we are to claim authority over our own lives. An important next step for queer people is to show greater discernment
in choosing those to whom we hand the reins of religious authority.
Although it is true that queerphobic religious leaders tend to dominate the news, they do not in fact speak for the entirety of their
traditions. It is imperative for progressive Christians to become

much more visible and audible in our proclamation of a robust, queer-positive gospel. But it would help immeasurably if those whose well-being is at stake would affirm the authenticity of that message. When LGBTQ people casually assert that Christianity is inherently queerphobic, we give power to the faux pious who argue, wrongly, that Christianity is inherently queerphobic! This renders queer Christians invisible, and our entire community suffers as a result.

Being queer and Christian is not easy. It's very easy at an interior level, because the two paths are so resonant. But politically, socially, it's a narrow road. And that's coming from a white cisgender American woman who enjoys a host of privileges. Imagine what it's like for a queer Christian in, say, Nigeria, who is struggling to be heard. Davis Mac-Iyalla is a gay man and activist from Nigeria who is also a devout Anglican. In 2009 Mac-Iyalla wrote an open letter to the archbishop of Canterbury, spiritual leader of the Anglican Communion. He called on the archbishop and all of the primates (leaders of the various national churches in our communion) to reject queerphobic appeals to religion, particularly those used to advance violent legislation:

> The anti-homosexuality legislation proposed and enacted
> in Uganda and many other former British colonies has
> caused misery for many lesbian, gay, bisexual and trans-
> gendered people, many of whom are forced to flee their
> countries due to this persecution. Religion is often cited
> as a justification for state and non-state violence against
> LGBT people. As a gay refugee from Nigeria who has
> faced this persecution, I am well aware of the misery
> LGBT people can go through in Africa. As a practising
> Anglican Christian, I believe it is crucial that the Anglican
> Communion unites to prevent the killing of people on
> the grounds of sexuality.[4]

Mac-Iyalla is doing in this letter what queer Christians need to be doing more of in general: he is raising his voice and demanding to be heard—at significant cost to himself. Those of us who are queer and Christian have a particular obligation to proclaim a gospel that is attuned to intersectional and hybrid realities. We are doubly called, as queers and as Christians, to insist that the churches and the LGBTQ communities we call home acknowledge us in all our complexity and respect the authenticity of our witness.

AUTHENTICITY IN CHRISTIAN COMMUNITY:
A HEALTHY APPROACH TO SELF AND OTHER

Being truthful about yourself in all your complexity is essential to authentic human connection. If you aren't honest about who you are, it limits your ability to participate honestly in human interactions and hobbles the ability of others to engage you authentically. Finding authentic connection in community thus demands both that you tell the truth about yourself and that you help build spaces where others can do the same.

The draw of authentic human connection is powerful. It is perhaps the most important reason that anyone chooses to join a faith community. Now, maybe you go to church sometimes just to hear exquisite music. Maybe you need stillness. Maybe you have children and you want them to learn the basics of a faith tradition. These are all solid reasons to go to church. But church membership is about more than this.

Christian community should be a place where one gets to work out the most vexing ethical challenge of our lives: the challenge to perceive and negotiate a healthy relationship between Self and Other.

Doing this well is hard work, and it is the rare church that really takes this part of our mission seriously. Some do. I was blessed early in my adult life to join a church where the priest constantly reminded us that "church is not a club; you don't get to choose the members, nor do I." This church was a place where many of us were wounded. We didn't always agree, and our disagreements sometimes became pitched precisely because there were a lot of raw feelings exposed whenever conflicts arose. My priest's refrain, that we had to work it out with each other because that is what church demands, really stuck with me. And when I finally became a priest, it informed my understanding of what community life was supposed to be about.

I was ordained in 2006 and was called to be the Episcopal chaplain to Northwestern University. I had always wanted to do college chaplaincy, and to have that dream fulfilled was nothing short of a miracle to me.

My family and I arrived in Evanston at the beginning of the 2006–2007 academic year. It was a time of controversy inside the Episcopal Church. Just three years earlier, General Convention, our national legislative body, had approved the consecration of Gene Robinson to be the first openly gay bishop in the Anglican Communion, our global family of faith. There was tumult throughout the communion, and sharp dissension within the American church about whether we had gone too far by treading onto territory that was so uncomfortable for so many people in our church.

My ministry at Canterbury Northwestern was not immune to the tide of controversy. There were several conservative students who were struggling with the decision to approve Bishop Robinson's consecration. There were also several progressive students who thought it was a great thing for the larger church. These students were friends who had already begun the difficult work of talking with each other—respectfully, with love—in order to try to understand one another's perspectives. That they agreed unanimously to call me, an out lesbian in a covenanted relationship with another woman, was no small leap of faith for the more conservative students in the ministry.

The ripples of dissension notwithstanding, our sense that we belonged together was strong, and we set out to create a spiritual home where we could bring our full selves to bear, and together, try to find God in our communal life. Years later one of the students, Jenn, described what the community felt like to her:

> My first two years [at Canterbury] significantly shaped my idea of what a vibrant, thriving church community should be. It was intimate and personally accountable, it was safe and supportive, it was woven into every day and area of our lives, it was open to hard questions and skepticism, it looked trustingly to the Holy Spirit, and relied on prayer, worship, and fellowship to center our communal as well as personal lives. There was a deeply human quality and authenticity to it all; there were occasional tensions or

jealousies and all the emotions that inhere in otherwise happy families, but looking back I see our existence at the time as a sustained miracle, a gift of the Holy Spirit.[5]

Many of the key ingredients for a healthy community were already present in this community when I arrived. What I brought with me was my deep love of scripture, an ability to lead vibrant worship, and importantly, the queer insights that I've been discussing in these chapters. Having experienced people bringing their full selves to bear in queer community—sometimes duking it out, but always with a larger sense of identity and purpose—I was able to help these brilliant and largely self-aware college students bring their hearts and minds into constructive conversation. Together, we built a community of extraordinary faith and vibrancy.

And then I lost my mooring. Over the course of my second year at Canterbury I found myself falling in love with one of the graduate students who had made our community her spiritual home. There is no simple answer to the question of whether I regret the connection we forged. Despite the moral and ethical and emotional complexity, it was one of the most significant relationships of my life, and it shaped me profoundly. Still, I would give almost anything to be able to go back and navigate the whole thing differently.

Frightened by a situation that I didn't know how to handle, I handled it badly. It took me way too long to disclose my feelings to anyone. I didn't seek help or advice. My relationship with my partner had already begun to fray, and I let it unravel. We broke up; I moved out. I disclosed to my community the end of that relationship and within a few scant weeks the existence of another, one that had been developing under their noses but that I had kept from them. My board, unnerved, went into lockdown and voted to dismiss me almost immediately.

To say that it was a mess is beyond understatement. The fallout left many of us shattered. The lives of people I love deeply, including my children, were painfully upended. It took me years to put my life and my priesthood back together.

The reason I'm writing this is to tell you what happened to the students who were left behind to clean up the mess inside the community. You see, they were really committed to all that work we had done to be honest and authentic with each other. And they stayed committed to it even after I, supposedly the standard bearer, had this massive lapse, failing over a period of months to be honest and authentic with them.

As you can imagine, the community was torn by anger, conflicted loyalties, and raw pain. After I was completely out of the picture, the diocese brought in a mediator to help reconcile the factions that had emerged and were duking it out. I am told that the mediator asked the students to talk to her rather than cross talk with each other. The rules, I am told, felt intrusive to students who wanted to engage each other in dialogue. And then what Jenn had described as a "gift of the Holy Spirit" again took hold:

> What happened in the aftermath of the meeting (as immediately as ten minutes later, cleaning up the coffee and snacks we had laid out) was not accidental at all. *We intentionally turned ourselves first individually toward the Holy Spirit, and then together toward the problem.* That is when the unsuccessful conflict resolution was abandoned and the conflict transformation began. Earlier, many of us acknowledged we had prayed for God to stop the conflict, to heal the wounds and restore equilibrium to our community—in desperation we had just begged Him to stop the pain. We had not come before God, broken, asking Him to guide us individually as He willed, to submit ourselves to the Holy Spirit and not demand easy answers and resolution we were not ready for yet. Real, open communication tore scabs off wounds that had festered, but the flood of talking that happened over the following days was like a salve.

Jenn writes that in the conversation that followed, students realized that "opposing" perspectives were more similar than they had previously allowed, that there were wounds on both sides that had not previously been seen by the others, and that the commitment to keeping the community running—by everyone—was stronger than they had realized but demanded more help from people who had slipped to the margins when the storm hit. The pivotal shift came when students stopped focusing on their feelings for/about me, and started taking responsibility for their relationships to the community and to each other. She continues:

> One of the most difficult parts of the process of reconcili-ation was acknowledging and confessing the ways we had been unhelpful, petty, unfair and spiteful. This practice of reflection and humility led to enormous spiritual growth in certain members of the community, myself included. Open communication revealed fairly similar views of what transpired, that people, despite siding with a "group" when polarization occurred, were really ambivalent. The next step in repentance is to resolve not to continue sinning; the transformation continued in the realization that organiza-tional dynamics had to change in order for the community to achieve our common future visioning of rebuilding, welcoming an interim priest, and recruiting new members in the coming academic year. The community encouraged students who felt left out of the leadership to begin new ministries, take over existing ones, and apply for Board membership. This was an important step toward resolv-ing longstanding resentments over access and power in the organization and uneven distribution of workload.

I am not proud of my behavior; but I am fiercely proud of those young adults. What Jenn is describing here is Christian community at its level best.

This is what we are called to as a church. This level of honesty and work—this is what you are called to be and do as someone on the Christian path. I hope that you never have to deal with a mess like the one I made for these students, but you and I both know that every community has its messes. And honestly, it is in putting on your waders, pulling out the mops, and working together in the muck that some of the most important work of our lives gets done.

This is the work of touching and being touched. This is how any one of us puts ourselves in the path of *naga*, God's exquisite touch that wounds and heals, that destroys and saves. As Jenn describes so well, this work involves a complex dynamic in which the individual comes to terms with herself, which makes it possible for the entire community to move forward. A person may invest in such a process out of self-interest, out of concern for her own spiritual health. In truth, though, it is very common for the motivation to go the other way: preserving the group can be a powerful incentive for an individual to engage this work, for reasons that have everything to do with the mysterious power of our relational God. Ultimately, if you do the work, it doesn't matter whether you come to it out of concern for yourself or the community or, hopefully, both. Shoring up one with integrity will shore up the other.

Queer people know that living out our identities calls us to find others who share those identities, and to create spaces where we can be ourselves together with some measure of safety, inviting others into those spaces and using them as a base of operations to reach out to others who need us. Because we need one another so much, there is a level of accountability to each other that many of us seem to grasp and shoulder intuitively.

For Christians, accountability to one another is an explicit demand of our tradition. "By this everyone will know that you are my disciples," said Jesus, "if you have love for one another."[6] As we have discussed several times, "love" in the Christian sense has everything to do with communities that people enter deliberately, and build up with perseverance.

Thus commitment to Christian community is not merely a sign of our faith; it is a crucial component of both the path we are on and the message that we preach. The Gospel of a theologically substantive God is proclaimed both by individuals and by the community as a whole, and doing so takes courage. You have to be rooted in a community that is rigorous in demonstrating love and accountability to one another. Both the love and the accountability themselves model the theological substance of the Gospel: thus the theology of our tradition and the ethics we live reinforce each other and depend upon each other.[7]

This is the fundamental problem with the inclination to live out your faith life in solitude, without the discipline of a tradition or community—what some people describe as "spiritual but not religious." Living the ethical life demanded by God is so greatly facilitated by relationships with others that it is honestly hard to see how one can truly manage it alone. And no matter how ethical your life, there is still something important that is missing if you aren't living it out in intentional community that you have deliberately entered and claimed, and to which you have committed yourself.

At the same time, individual churches don't necessarily cultivate the kind of authenticity and accountability to the Other that Jenn and the students in her community demanded of themselves. Many churches cultivate responsibility—for outreach ministries, for liturgy, for church governance—and that is important. But responsibility for specific duties is not the same thing as the kind of accountability to one another that fosters spiritual growth.

There are churches that do this well. If you are looking for a church, I encourage you to look for one that breeds healthy interpersonal dynamics. Look for a place where members know themselves (themSelves), and treat each Other with respect. Look for a community that corporately knows ItSelf and engages in a healthy way with Others. I hope that's already on your short list of things that you might be seeking—but know that you are right to expect it in a Christian community. If you are already in a community, I encourage you to dedicate yourself to a discipline of healthy Self/Other dynamics. If you are a leader, demand it of yourself and among the others leading ministries for which you have responsibility.

Here are some of the ways that a Christian community can and should incarnate healthy Self/Other dynamics.

Power in a Christian community should be shared, and shared broadly. There are always some decisions that are properly made by a small or elected group, and in rare instances there are decisions that are appropriately made in confidential settings. But to the maximum extent possible, decisions should be made prayerfully (I mean that literally—people joining in prayer together), through conversation and group deliberation that works to include rather than exclude church members.

I am not naïve about power dynamics or ignorant of political processes. Intermingled with my years in professional ministry, I have enjoyed a robust career as a professional political strategist. I am good at it, precisely because I understand how people use power to pursue their self-interest—and because I know how to do that myself. I know the fine art of moving behind the scenes, convincing people to see my group's side of a dispute, brokering deals, and building up a critical mass of votes to move my group's issue/contract/funding proposal down the field. I also know the more laborious art of grassroots education, coalition building, and intragroup dialogue. I tell you: the church should always be more about the latter than the former.

Although I am a skilled political operative, I'm lousy at church politics. Over the years I have often pondered why church politics is so different, so difficult for me. I think the answer is fairly simple: in the professional political world, people are up front about the facts that 1) we are engaged in politics, and 2) we each have a vested interest in the outcome. All too often in the church, people play politics but pretend that we are doing something else—usually something having to do with an alleged greater good, or God's will, or something like that.

Church politics would be a whole lot less ugly if people were more honest about the fact that we have self-interest and if we had open dialogue about what those interests are and why they matter so much to us. There is no crime in having a vested interest in the outcome of a decision. The crime, so to speak, comes when you fail to acknowledge that interest—to yourself or to others—or worse, hotly deny it. Such denial prevents the community from talking openly about the dynamics that are probably operating most powerfully beneath the surface of decisions both momentous and mundane.

Open and honest conversation is crucial to any healthy relational process, but it is particularly important to a community of faith. Being honest about one's interests, one's fears, one's authentic perspective is crucial to negotiating the relationship between Self and Other with the health that faith life demands.

One of the biggest mistakes I made at Canterbury was that I shut everyone in the community out of my process—even though every person in the community was going to be affected by the decisions I was struggling to make. I did this out of fear, and out of deep mistrust that anyone else would help us all move forward to a place of health.[8] If I could change just one thing that I did during that time, this is what I would change. Keeping power to myself caused me to lose the ethical perspective I had always relied on, both as a lesbian and as a Christian. That ethic demands rigorous engagement with others as modus operandi, keeping the health of the community and of one's other personal relationships in view. Adhering to my queer/Christian ethic would also have helped me attend to my own well-being. Keeping power to myself prevented people from helping *me*, at a time when I was drowning and needed a lifeline.

The fear that I was feeling is, I think, not uncharacteristic of what causes many people of good heart to shut others out. Sometimes people in churches usurp decision making not because they are evil power mongers, but because they think they know the right way to go forward and they are afraid that a broader conversation will lead to the wrong decision. But let's be honest: there are also plenty of people who do hoard power, just to do it, for a myriad of reasons. Failing to be honest about our self-interest in church creates fields that are ripe for the abuse of power, toxic to healthy relational dynamics, and disastrous for a community's ability to perceive God in its midst.

Christian community can't thrive like that. Fear, secrecy, and power hoarding too effectively undermine the core principles of trust and reliance on one another that are at the heart of our faith. We know ourselves to be reliant on God; deliberately relying on others is one of the ways that we practice our reliance on God and, prayerfully, can come to trust more and more deeply both in God and in one another.

And here it matters to acknowledge that when the institutional church itself gets it wrong, the price is very high. I know that I bear a lot of responsibility for what went wrong at Canterbury, but I also know that I would not have been as afraid as I was had I not over the years been badly injured by church dynamics that failed to treat queer lives and relationships with care and respect. If the church is going to demand accountability and honesty from its clergy—and the church is correct to do so—then the church itself needs both to model such accountability and to cultivate environments that respect and value the human beings who inhabit them, in all our diversity.

Church community should be a place where we work hard to see and respect each other as we really are. We talked earlier about intersectionality and hybridity, people's experiences of possessing multiple identities, some of which communicate privilege and some of which leave one vulnerable to oppression. The truth is, we are all complicated beings. Most of us experience layers of privilege and pain—some of which are visible to others and many of which are not. Church should not ever be a place where people get the message that they can't disclose their true selves, nor a place where disclosing one's true self puts one in peril.

It is our job to listen for, respect, and seek to comprehend people's identities and experiences in all their multiplicity. In Christian community, difference is not a problem to be overcome; it is a strength that is crucial to our call. In the First Letter to the Corinthians, Paul likens the community to a human body:

> Indeed, the body does not consist of one member but of many. If the foot would say, "Because I am not a hand, I do not belong to the body," that would not make it any less a part of the body. . . . But as it is, God arranged the members in the body, each one of them, as [Ze] chose. If all were a single member, where would the body be? As it is, there are many members, yet one body. The eye cannot say to the hand, "I have no need of you," nor again the head to the feet, "I have no need of you."[9]

Paul's message is explicit: we don't need one another simply to increase our numbers; we need others within the community to be *different* from ourselves. This is one of the most important and explicit ways that Paul characterizes a healthy relationship between Self and Other, insisting that all Christians appreciate just how vital the difference inherent in the Other is to our lives and to the cosmic project of which we are now a part.

It is our privilege to find ways to grow from that diversity—to embrace that these different identities and different levels of privilege inform not just the other person's experience of sacred truth, but yours as well. Work to take these different identities/experiences into account in your community. Let these dynamics inform your interior conversations. If you belong to a church, understand the power that you already have simply by being a member—the one who already exists in the place that a visitor has to enter for the first time. Be aware of tendencies to keep power to a few, to shut others out of decision making, to assume that you can evaluate anyone else's identities or beliefs based on whom they appear to be. Use what you learn and apply those lessons to your church's work in the world. Whose voices are being heard? Whose voices aren't? How many layers of identity are being recognized, valued, and drawn upon for discernment?

Queering lines of power in this way could help churches navigate some of our most vexing problems. In recent years many Protestant denominations have paid keen attention to the de facto racial segregation that is all too common in our churches. In the United States, much of this segregation is historically rooted in denominational or congregational schisms that were explicitly about race and power.[10] Some of it is rooted in cultural divides that raise complex logistical issues within liturgy, such as attempting to worship in multiple languages. Today, many predominantly white denominations have created offices specifically designed to support ministries by and/or for various ethnic groups, including offices for Hispanic, African American, and Asian ministries. The Presbyterian Church has a national office for "Intercultural Ministries," which sounds intriguingly like an effort to rupture walls that separate people along racial lines and allow new and innovative liturgical exploration to thrive.

Several denominations have launched efforts to recruit a more racially diverse pool of candidates for ordination. Ordaining people of color and giving them pulpits—especially people of color who possess a strong sense of how their racial identity informs their faith—has in some places proven a successful path for addressing de facto segregation. Queer clergy of color often possess extraordinary gifts for seeing how to queer lines of race, cultural heritage, and language in order to create worship experiences and communities that are pulsing with life. The potential benefit to Christianity in raising up such gifted ministers is significant, but it will be reaped only if churches give these clerics the opportunity to work and have their backs when they bring themselves authentically to the altar.

Whether the issue is empowerment of people who have been historically marginalized, or simply the challenge for any one of us to bring our most closely guarded selves to bear, authenticity in church requires courage. It is hard work to talk openly when you are afraid of losing something you value or need. It can be hard to trust, hard to be honest, hard to put yourself at risk of attack. You know all of this. But the fact that it is hard does not excuse churches from doing the work. In fact, church should be the place where we take most seriously the need to do this and to do it well. The challenge inherent in the relationship between Self and Other exists in every sphere of our lives. Church should be the place where we get to work it out. Church should be the place where our priesthood shows forth, where we make ourselves vulnerable—as individuals and as communities—to invite both individuals and other kinds of communities to enter the sacred.

The call to authenticity is an end in itself in Christian community, but it also leads us to the water's edge of Christian mission. Grappling honestly with the real lives of real people puts each of us keenly in touch with an interior imperative to pay close attention to the needs of those on the margins. This is the ethical call that plunges us deep into scandal.

CHAPTER 10

HOSPITALITY

Queer people throw excellent parties. Some of our most important parties are our Pride celebrations, which become more fabulous with every new person who attends. We want as many people at those parties and marches and protests as possible, not least because the more people who are there, the stronger we feel and the stronger our community becomes.

Pride is shot through with an ethic of hospitality. Hospitality is the business of receiving guests and making them feel welcome. These guests may be travelers who are seeking shelter, or food. They may have been invited to dinner, or to a celebration. They may be people who need protection of some kind. They may be family members, friends, or complete strangers. A posture of hospitality begins before anyone has arrived, and entails preparedness for those whom one does not know to anticipate. Once guests are present, hospitality involves a proactive impulse to see what people need and to provide it. A good host is alert to hir guests, observes their needs, and responds generously and appropriately.

More broadly, an ethic of hospitality guides transactions between Self and Other. If you are from a culture that takes hospitality seriously—and many do—you know that the rules of hospitality apply not just to hosts (Self) but also to guests (Other). There's a way in which one is rather constantly assuming one of these two positions, host or guest, and is having to navigate the ethical norms that pertain to whichever position one is in.

Healthy Pride makes authentic hospitality possible, because Pride encompasses two levels of awareness that are crucial to hospitality: first, awareness of human value, both one's own and others';

and second, awareness of our connection to and dependence upon one another.

Queer people have a visceral instinct for hospitality, which is inherently incarnational. Hospitality involves meeting needs that are bodily and often fairly intimate: what you eat, when you eat it, and who shares your food; where you sleep, when you sleep, and yes, sometimes, who shares your bed.

This means that hospitality, like queerness, has to deal constantly with an awareness of scandal. When the awareness is conscious, a person navigating hospitality has to decide where the traps are set, whether she or her guests might be snared in them, and how she feels about the danger.

In the 1980s and '90s many people, queer and nonqueer, rushed to bedsides and into hospitals to care for people with HIV/AIDS. The decision to provide hospitality came at no small cost. I knew a nurse who was forbidden to hold her newborn nephew because his parents were afraid she would infect him just by virtue of her proximity to AIDS patients. The fears had absolutely nothing to do with a realistic assessment that transmission of the virus was a risk; it had everything to do with people on the front lines being "tainted" by their association with a medical condition that frightened or even scandalized others.

Queer people have long dived willingly into scandal for the sake of hospitality. We do so in our parties, and we do so when we care for people on the margins. We also do so in our political activism.

In October 1995, Pope John Paul II came to New York City. I sat in on a meeting at which several AIDS activists planned an action to protest John Paul's position on condom use, which in their eyes put millions of lives at risk. Those were the days of direct action, protests carefully choreographed and scripted to achieve maximum media attention. We needed a chant that would succinctly state the problem and be short, snappy, and rhythmic. People started tossing out ideas, which quickly devolved into angry caricatures of John Paul's person. Finally, one man in the group asked to be heard. "I understand your anger. I do. This pope is terrible on our issues. But he is doing more to call attention to extreme poverty than anyone else I know. His work is important, and it is important to me. I won't participate in disparaging him as a human being." Silence fell in the room. I had no idea what was going to happen next.

It took courage for this man to speak. So many of our people were dying. It felt like war. There were Catholic hospitals on the forefront of caring for people with HIV/AIDS, but the Vatican continued to issue statements disparaging queer identity and denying the efficacy of the most basic vehicles for stopping transmission of the virus. There was truth in this man's statement; but for those of us dealing with the fallout of Vatican condemnation, defending the pope was scandalous. Would we respect this man in our midst, respect the marginalized people for whom he was speaking? Or would we be offended by him, and cast him out? When we started up again, the tone had completely changed. I doubt that a single person changed hir opinion about the pope, but we all allowed ourselves to be affected by this man's witness. I saw this over and over again in meetings where people were organizing direct actions: the ability of queer activists to see one another and hold with respect our complex concerns, our intersectional identities. This man called us out on the risk of insularity, demanding that we also see the people living in poverty across the globe, and that we respect the interconnection among experiences of marginalization.

Queer people often understand that advancing our self-interest includes advancing the well-being of people whom we may not yet perceive to be part of "us." That's because many of us are aware of our complex identities and the intersectional dynamics at work. Being aware of our intersectionality means that when we "look to the margins," we know that we are often looking around right here in the room where we're sitting. We aren't looking "over there" at "those people." We know, therefore, that we have strength even as we inhabit marginal space. We know that we have power that can be used to make life more possible for folks who are barely surviving on the margin, right here in our midst.

That's why our definition of "us" is ever expanding. We are keenly aware that we are part of a larger movement. We are a people who, at our best, always have a vision in view—a vision in which life is better, more possible, for each of us, and for all of us. We know that our ability to move forward is dependent on our ability to see people who are on the margins. including ourselves, and weave them—us—into the fold. Our needs as individuals and our needs as a community sometimes exist in tension, but they constantly inform each other and constantly serve as check and balance in our ethical deliberation.

HOSPITALITY: HEALTHY ESCHATOLOGY

A great deal of theological thinking is fiercely imaginative. One of the theological questions that demands an imaginative response is this: Where are we going? I don't mean "tonight," or "this weekend," or even "next summer." I mean, *ultimately*. Where are we—as a people, as sentient beings in this universe—headed? This question draws us into the realm of eschatology.

Eschatology is the study of "the end times." That's what the Greek literally means. Eschatology keeps us looking to the future for . . . something. It bears a relationship to but is not the same thing as apocalypticism, which is the expectation that the world will end in destruction. Progressive Christians often have virtually no idea what to do with these ideas because, along the running theme of this book, they are in theological territory that has largely been hijacked to advance causes that we progressives find offensive.

Queer theologian Elizabeth Stuart argues that eschatology is important not because by talking about it we can figure out exactly what heaven is like, but rather because our visioning tells us "a great deal about our current values and aspirations."[1] Such discourses, she argues,

> are spaces where we dare to dream impossible dreams,
> where language cracks and the divine presence may seep
> through. . . . Like Jesus' parables, which were eschato-
> logical in content, eschatological discourse makes room
> for God by cracking "the deep structure of our accepted
> world."

Eschatology speaks of our destiny, and our destination. How do we know where we are going if we have given up dreaming about what it will be like when we get there?

Eschatology is deeply embedded in early church understandings of what Christianity is all about. It is woven through our scripture. And, as Stuart suggests, it has practical impact on the work that we do. Revealing both our understanding of ourselves and our dreams, eschatology should inform our decisions about the actions we take that are designed to make the world a better place, a place that somehow manifests God's realm on earth.

We have been talking about the relationship between theology and ethics. We have observed that theology and ethics work together, that in a sense, they make each other possible. Eschatology asks us foundational questions about why we do justice work at all. Are we building a better world simply to demonstrate our faith, because Jesus told us to do it? Or does something in all that action actually accomplish something that is important to God, and to us? To put it another way: Are we simply walking this path, or are we paving it as we go?

Jürgen Moltmann is a German theologian who in the mid-twentieth century pushed liberal Christianity to take eschatology more seriously as a lens for comprehending our purpose.

Drawing on the scriptural concept of *adventus*—the God "who is and who was and who is to come"[2]—Moltmann asserted that God is not a static being, a final destination for humanity, but rather that God is a dynamic presence who is actively moving toward us from the future, empowering us forward. Thus, Moltmann wrote, God becomes the ground for our freedom and "the ground of the transformation of the world."[3]

What Moltmann describes is a very queer idea, and I include in that phrase an appreciation for one of the early definitions of queer: it is strange, puzzling. I have spent years trying to comprehend—trying to imagine—what it means for God to be coming at us from the future. Moltmann begs remarkable questions about our relationship to time, about the meaning of human progress. His idea is also queer because he is suggesting that there is a binary at work in human experience of *now* and *then*—a binary that God ruptures decisively.

By queering perceived separations between now and the future, eschatology dramatically informs both the ministries we take on and, significantly, our approach to those ministries. Eschatology answers the basic question, "Why do we do outreach ministries anyway?" with a much richer answer than, "Because Jesus said to."

Eschatology helps frame our work not as "service to people who are not Us," but rather as "looking to the margins to see and be in relationship with those whom I have not yet perceived or acknowledged, to meet needs that will bring us into a new understanding of who We are."

Churches often characterize this work as "service" or "outreach," but "looking to the margins" is a better description of what happens in queer community. The queer community rarely looks around, as churches sometimes do, to say, "We should help some people. Whom should we help?" Rather, in queer community we tend to hear the cry of someone inside the community who is in pain, and many of us respond. Our human response is in some ways resonant with the action God takes in Hebrew scripture when Ze goes into action because Ze has "observed the misery of my people" and "heard their cry."[4]

Thus as the new millennium set in we finally began to pay attention to the voices of trans* people whose identities and needs had long been shoved aside. Thus we began to pay attention to the plight of runaway and homeless youth. Thus have attempts to name our community evolved, from "gay" to "gay and lesbian" to "lesbian, gay, and bisexual" to "LGBT" and on and on to a veritable alphabet of specific identities and experiences. Growing awareness of the need to invite people onto that list proactively was one of the factors that eventually led many of us to embrace the word "queer" as something of an umbrella term—and an infrastructural identity. That history, from "gay" to "queer" itself, says a lot about our ethical path: the work that we do is shot through with a deep awareness of our queer connection, while it simultaneously shakes up our comprehension of who we are and how we are distinct from one another.

One does not need to be queer to be able to perceive what this movement feels like. Human migration has a similar trajectory and ultimately demands a similar response. People seeking refuge, asylum, or simply a better life for their children set out for a new land. Those who are already in that land may be welcoming or hostile, but eventually "the immigrant" becomes part of the cultural landscape. "They" become "us." Some of the most interesting social justice work being done in the United States today involves listening to the voices of young people who live in that liminal, transitional space between us and them: the Dreamers, for instance, many of whom have lived most of their lives in this country and regardless of their documentation are as culturally American as any of their peers in school.[5]

Those of us who listen to these voices, queer and nonqueer, understand that our awareness of others will shape our understanding of ourselves and will shape the work that we know we must do, as we live into the future that calls us forward, as we strive to be a community that will continue to grow in strength, in numbers, and in integrity.

In this way, queer ethics seems intuitively to mirror something of Moltmann's eschatology with a clarity that can be helpful to progressive Christians.[6] Envisioning God as one coming toward us from the future enhances the meaning of the queer/Christian path we are on. The path is not just a discipline that leads to meaning, (ethics leading to theology), but it is in a way an emanation of God-self. The path itself is an encounter with the God who is coming toward us.

The challenge for ministries that work toward justice is to be deeply cognizant of how the work itself articulates and manifests a healthy awareness of dynamics between Self and Other, making it possible for more people to walk the path on which we encounter the living God. "Justice" can be defined broadly. Justice ministries might focus on food insecurity, or housing, or health care, or extreme poverty, or climate change, or political/religious/economic persecution, or . . . the list goes on. The term "justice" is intrinsically relational, whether it is being discussed in scripture or in a court of law. That's why framing it as part of the work of hospitality is so deeply correct. Whatever you are called to address, wherever your heart and body are going to show up to work, be sure to go there with a strong sense of who you are and what your stake is in the relationship with the Self/Other you are going to encounter.

There are many progressive churches that take these questions and dynamics seriously. Social justice ministry is something progressive Christianity often does well. It is the place where many Christians have worked hard to comprehend a healthy relationship between Self and Other, such as by supporting immigrants and providing safe havens for refugees. This ethic deeply informs contemporary international outreach as work that is fundamentally about solidarity, partnership, and relationship building.

We prioritize this kind of social justice work as an essential part of our mission, and it often manifests robust and gracious hospitality. It is, in fact, a starting point for many progressive Christians and communities, a way to enter into a deeper understanding of our faith and of God. If you are one of those people, and if you were writing this book, maybe you would have written these chapters on ethics in a different order. Maybe instead of starting with the section on "Pride," you would have started with "Looking to the Margins." You could make a strong argument for doing just that.

The most authentic social justice ministries exact a price even as they cultivate joy. That's because hospitality requires that one confront scandal. We have looked at numerous biblical passages in which Jesus had to deal with being scandalous or scandalized. What we didn't talk about were the many passages in which Jesus scandalized his contemporaries simply by occupying the same space as people who were considered unclean. And he didn't just occupy the space—he touched people. Touching someone who is considered unclean means you get contaminated—ritualistically, socially, and sometimes physiologically as well. This means that Jesus took on the state of being unclean, and he took on whatever stigma was applied to the people he was engaging: women, children, Samaritans, lepers, you name it. In other words, Jesus's work meant that he constantly scandalized people by becoming a scandal to them. And he did this at the exact moment when he was doing the kinds of work that Christians are often trying to emulate when we engage in outreach or social justice ministries.

Where is the scandal in your work? What pressure exists to dispense with it? To the extent that your work is scandalous to others, how willing are you to enter and own the scandal of it? If your work is completely "safe," why is that? It is common for people of privilege to feel "unsafe" when we enter into spaces that are decrepit or engage with people who are sick or hungry or haven't bathed or whatever. It's worth figuring out how and why feelings of safety get stirred up in those situations, but those feelings are not a sufficient barometer for assessing your work. When it comes to scandal, being "unsafe" means a whole lot more than just "it makes me uncomfortable to be around people like that."

Facing down scandal means rupturing binaries that do violence to people, both conceptually and in practical life. Right in line with what queer people comprehend, it means *understanding the scandal that you, as a Christian, already are.* We Christians are called to look to the margins, knowing that we already exist there: it is the space we inhabit. This is one of the most important reasons that we have to come out, understand our intersectional identities, and name ourselves as scandalous: we have to queer the lines between "those people over there" who are on the margins, who are scandalous, and "us" sitting in whatever marginalized/privileged space we occupy.

This kind of queering gives offense to others, especially to people who want to stay safely in their privileged world, whether on the Left or on the Right. This kind of queering scandalizes, and if it doesn't, it isn't doing an important part of its job.

But remember that the scandal itself is part of our eschatological vision. An awareness of scandal helps clarify some of the most vexing Self/Other dynamics that we humans face. By looking to the margin and claiming our place there we allow ourselves to be called together, rupturing the binary of those who are in and those who are out. We stand together, imagining God in our midst, undermining the power of false scandal by putting away the trap for good. The ethic and discipline of hospitality confronts scandal, shows the lie of the false binary, and makes our eschatological vision possible. In the doing of justice, ethics and theology work together so closely that the lines are almost queered. The vision and the work so reinforce each other, so thoroughly depend on each other, that they are nearly inseparable. Without one, neither is truly viable. With both, we may just find ourselves treading on a solid path, toward the God who is rushing to meet us.

CONCLUSION

A WILD, RECKLESS DREAM OF LOVE

On Palm Sunday, 2014, I went to church at St. Mark's in the Bowery in lower Manhattan. Winnie Varghese, the rector, a queer priest whose prophetic voice gives me hope for the church, quietly preached a sermon so powerful that it felt like my soul had been grasped and shaken.

Palm Sunday is a fiercely challenging day. This is the day when Jesus strides into Jerusalem, hailed by his followers. Within a week, he will be killed. Winnie gazed unflinchingly upon this day in all its complexity—all of its hope, all of its impending violence. "When there was a parade [in Jesus's time]," she said, "it was Rome coming in to show them they were conquered, that their God had been humiliated, that they would never be free. And Jesus comes in looking like David . . ."[1] She reminded us that for these people, living this moment, there was no cozy postscript to soften the violence he was about to face. "This is not a bunch of people thinking resurrection comes at the end of this week":

> In that little moment before he dies—they don't know
> how many days it will be, but they know he will die—
> they just celebrate their freedom. Now hear it, because
> no freedom has happened. They are not any more free
> than the day before or the day before, but they have in this
> brief moment—as we have in this brief moment—a little
> bit of a vision of what the reign of God might look like.
> That a gentle, healing, wise man, in the position of the
> prophets, enraged by injustice against women and children
> and his people and the sick and the outsider, that this one
> could be a sign of God's reign now. That this might be

who we are. And the people respond with this glorious procession, every one of them potentially marking themselves also for death by Rome.

These are people who have hope—hope as a kind of knowledge of themselves, knowledge of an identity that cannot be crushed:

> They risk themselves to sing aloud a memory of who
> they knew they could be because God had told them
> they could be those people: the chosen, the beloved,
> the wildly inclusive, those believing that all of creation
> were vessels made to be good forever and whole, not
> shattered, as they were and were about to be again.

I have written that my faith in the Christian gospel is not based on someone drumming it into my head, nor on my confidence that it all makes rational sense. Rather, my faith in the gospel is based on the fact that I experience it to be true. There are two places where I have most deeply experienced the truth that Winnie describes here—the wild, reckless dream of a life where love truly reigns: in the narrative of Jesus's final days in Jerusalem, and in my experience of queer community. Leslie Feinberg might have used language similar to Winnie's to describe a community of women who knew absolutely that violence was coming, but who went to the bars anyway, who dressed the way they needed to dress anyway, because they knew who they were and they knew that they needed to be those people, together: "They risk themselves to sing aloud a memory of who they knew they could be."

What happens on Palm Sunday is important for myriad reasons. It matters that people come together *as a people* to remember who they are, and who they are meant to be. This happened for Jesus's followers on that day. It matters that people who live under repressive regimes demonstrate against coercive violence. It matters that people engage their bodies in proclaiming their desire for a better life. It matters that people live into hope. It matters that people proclaim aloud, with their hearts, minds, souls, and bodies: "We are creatures of infinite value. What is alive in us cannot be killed."

This book has explored the trajectory of two paths, queer and Christian. Our discussion has moved like this:

Discernment of identity leads individuals and communities to:

Risk the proclamation of that identity;

Touch others, despite risk to oneself;

Navigate the inevitable scandal;

Participate in communities that demand integrity within ourselves, require justice in our dealings with one another, and look to the margins to address individual/communal/global degradation and suffering.

Queer people live this path without talking a lot about it. I suspect many of us don't even see the virtue that is plainly at work among us. One primary purpose in writing this book is to lift up this path in a way that both queer people and Christians can see, encouraging all of us to acknowledge the virtue that is both demanded and made possible by the facts of queer life.

Another primary purpose is to offer queer virtue as a model for Christian faith. Precisely because queer virtue is so visible in our world—much as those gathered on that first Palm Sunday would have been shockingly visible to everyone around them—it provides a model that one can observe, ponder, and emulate. This is a model that could help Christians better understand how and why we live the way we do; but also, very importantly, it is a model that can help more of us proclaim our faith in words and deeds more powerfully, with greater consequence.

Our world is beset by vexing, terrifying iterations of violence, from income inequality to severe economic deprivation; from religious intolerance to radical religious militarism. We are confronted on a daily basis by violence both horrific and mundane: gruesome beheadings, the savage destruction of cultural heritage, and throughout the globe, families chased from their homes by people waving the profane banner of rigidly intolerant, nominally religious views.

The Christian tradition, along with other faith traditions that are based on a law of love, speaks deeply to the terrorizing violence that pervades our world. Yes, Christianity condemns murder outright—as do Judaism and Islam. Christianity joins other world religions in calling for peace, for justice, for basic human compassion. These ethical calls are important not least for their clarity and simplicity, and moderate/progressive voices are correct to draw upon these simple, clear ethical standards when we condemn acts of violence.

But there is more at work in these traditions than basic ethical statutes that, when applied to the real world, sometimes prove not to be so simple after all. Christian ethics are constructed upon a sophisticated and robust theological infrastructure. If Christians were better able to perceive and name the Self/Other dynamics that undergird our tradition; if we were able to stand inside our tradition and comprehend the ways that we are individually and corporately involved in these dynamics, I tell you: we would far more often know what to say about the violence that runs rampant in our world. We would far more often know how to lift our voices and position our bodies to refute violence. And we would far more effectively be able to locate ourselves among the vast numbers of good, loving people in our world who seek meaning, who need hope: the gritty, determined, scandalous hope that is the very marrow of our tradition.

Winnie Varghese's sermon emanates from the core of the gospel. The Jesus she describes is both gentle and enraged. The setting she evokes exudes a sense of menace, and of home. The people in the crowd are on fire with love, even as they look fear directly in the eye. This is a story about people who, in remembering who they are, also remember that who they are is greater and stronger than whatever violence may come their way.

This is a story about a God who shows up to stand with them, with us. This is a God who not only understands the depth of our joys and the immensity of our heartaches, but who also turns them into opportunities for us to touch one another, to be touched by God. This is a God who is very queer, indeed.

In our midst, this God has raised up priests, both lay and ordained: people who have an innate sense of the divine working in their lives. Among these priests are countless people who identify as queer, who possess an innate sense of the essential queerness of the divine. The church needs their witness, just as the world now desperately needs the church's authentically queer witness. The moment is upon us for the church to step boldly into this place of radical vulnerability—discerning and claiming our identity, risking, touching, facing down scandal, adopting and being adopted by one another—and in doing so, open pathways for people the world over who are clamoring to enter the sacred.

ACKNOWLEDGMENTS

A great many minds, hearts, and souls have made invaluable contributions to this work, thanks be first and foremost to God.

Immeasurable gratitude goes to Caroline Perry, my radiant spiritual companion over a course of years and frontline interlocutor throughout the writing of this book. Caroline put in countless hours sifting through my first drafts, peering into the text with her characteristic brilliance and vibrant faith, helping to clarify thoughts, and offering perspicacious edits toward the elusive and sometimes maddening goal of "concision." Her enthusiasm for this project was sustentative and very often entailed generous care both of me and of my children.

Michael Bacon is a visionary priest and steadfast friend who has long articulated the queerness of God and the sacred calling of queer people. Michael perceives the Spirit as a genuine force in our world, and he communicates Hir power and presence with galvanizing clarity. My determination to write this book was forged in the discernment, hope, and frequent hilarity of our weekly lunch dates.

Catherine Shugrue dos Santos brings her intellect, energy, and considerable heart to bear on a daily basis to make the lives of queer people better and safer, including my own. She has made important contributions both to this manuscript and to the vision that undergirds it. To her and to all my friends at the NYC Anti-Violence Project who journeyed with me as the book was taking shape: thank you for your insights, courage, and persistent witness to the power of resurrection.

Crucial support for this project came from OASIS, the LGBT ministry in the Episcopal Diocese of Newark, New Jersey. The

2014 Louie Crew Scholarship allowed me to take unpaid leave from my job to write. A year later, OASIS awarded a grant to fund production of several short films promoting core messages of *Queer Virtue*. These films were brought to life through the generous effort and substantial talent of Markie Hancock.

As one who thrives on vigorous engagement with strong dialogical partners, I could not have been more fortunate than to work with my gracious and gifted editors, Michael Bronski and Gayatri Patnaik. Both were unfailingly supportive of this project, even as they challenged me to broaden its vision and hone its language. Their knowledge, insight, and skill have made this a better book.

I am exceedingly grateful to numerous friends and colleagues who read early manuscripts and provided valuable feedback, including Dr. Louie Crew, Dr. Susan Gore, the Right Reverend Mark Beckwith, Canon Gregory Jacobs, Lori and Marybeth Knoth, Sheila Lewandowski, the Very Reverend Tracey Lind, Barbara Turk, Cathy Roth Miller, the Reverend Winnie Varghese, Jenn Cruickshank, and the Reverend Erik Soldwedel.

Several queer communities and faith communities have illuminated my thinking about these ideas in workshops, conversations, and responses to sermons. Special thanks to the board and staff of Hudson Pride Connections Center and to the beautifully queer young souls in HPCC's YouthConnect program, and to the congregations of St. Andrew & Holy Communion in South Orange and All Saints Episcopal Parish in Hoboken, New Jersey.

The world would be a far better place if all queer souls were supported by the love that my family ceaselessly shows me, long manifest in robust discussion of matters political and spiritual. I am particularly grateful to my siblings Katherine Edman, Jonathan Edman, Erin Washko, and Noel Bullard. Dann Washko, Paige Washko, and Rosalind Edman joined a memorable conversation one Brigantine morning that had a direct impact on chapter 8. My father, a man of deep and quiet faith, has taught me a great deal about spiritual communion that does not require words. To Jasper and Leo: you live the dream of binary-rupturing virtue in ways that make your mother unspeakably proud.

Over the years numerous scholars and preachers, queer and not queer, have informed my approach to scripture, and many of them are named in this book. One who is not named but whose imprint cannot be missed is Dr. Phyllis Trible, with whom it was my great privilege to study while a student at Union Theological Seminary. Her encouragement lasted well beyond the Hosea seminar in which she challenged me to wrestle deeply with scripture, assuring me that "the text will sustain it." Her wisdom has never failed. To Professor Trible, and to the prophets named herein whose profound love of scripture has allowed so many of us to glimpse the sacred, I bow with respect and gratitude.

NOTES

Introduction

1. See the author's note regarding pronoun usage in this book.
2. Queer theory is a field of critical theory that seeks to comprehend queer perspective and make public discourse about queer experience possible. Annamarie Jagose offers a useful primer on the topic in her book *Queer Theory: An Introduction* (New York: New York University Press, 1997).
3. The earliest followers of Jesus considered themselves to be part of Judaism. Within a few centuries the movement broke with Judaism, becoming its own discrete tradition; but the sacred texts of Judaism, in which the teachings of Jesus and Paul were rooted, remained foundational texts for Christianity. The Christian bible is thus composed of both Hebrew scripture, which the Christian tradition inherited from Judaism, and Greek scripture, which includes the Gospels, Epistles, the Acts of the Apostles, and the book of Revelation.
4. Please see the author's note regarding my careful use of this terminology. I deny the assumption that Christianity is inherently queerphobic and affirm the many progressive denominations that celebrate queer lives as part of their Christian call. I am gesturing here toward people who call themselves Christian and who proclaim what I would describe as a flawed iteration of Christianity.
5. Maya Angelou, *I Know Why the Caged Bird Sings* (New York: Bantam Books, 1971), 142–56.

Chapter 1: On the Inherent Queerness of Christianity

1. This point was established as a matter of orthodoxy at the Council of Chalcedon, 451 CE.
2. John 13:35.
3. 1 Cor. 13:7.

Chapter 2: Identity

1. Simone de Beauvoir, *The Second Sex* (New York: Knopf, 1952). See especially the introduction.

2. Andrew Solomon describes this as "horizontal identity" in *Far from the Tree: Parents, Children, and the Search for Identity* (New York: Scribner, 2012).

Chapter 3: Risk

1. Judith Butler explores this idea and posits the concept of "performativity" in her groundbreaking book *Gender Trouble: Feminism and the Subversion of Identity* (New York: Routledge, 1990).

2. Hannah Phillips succinctly unpacks these clerics' arguments, observing both the easy target that gender construction has been for conservative religious and political leaders and also the "deliberate intellectual laziness" that is involved in these attacks. "Democracy in a Clergyman's Attire? Gender and Catholicism in Poland," *Crossing the Baltic* (blog), September 9, 2014, http://crossingthebaltic.com/2014/09/09/democracy-in-a-clergymans-attire-gender-and-catholicism-in-poland/. Slawomir Sierakowski quotes a Polish bishop asserting that the "ideology of gender presents a threat worse than Nazism and Communism combined." "The Polish Church's Gender Problem," *New York Times*, January 26, 2014, http://www.nytimes.com/2014/01/27/opinion/sierakowski-the-polish-churchs-gender-problem.html?_r=0.

3. Asked about environmental concerns, Pope Francis spoke of "Herods" "that destroy, that plot designs of death, that disfigure the face of man and woman, destroying creation." "Let's think of the nuclear arms, of the possibility to annihilate in a few instants a very high number of human beings," he continued. "Let's think also of genetic manipulation, of the manipulation of life, or of the gender theory, that does not recognize the order of creation." Quoted in Joshua J. McElwee, "Francis Strongly Criticizes Gender Theory, Comparing It to Nuclear Arms," *National Catholic Reporter*, February 13, 2015.

4. Luke 17:33; Mark 8:36.

5. On February 25, 2014, CBC News posted an interactive graphic documenting the status of these laws: http://www.cbc.ca/news2/interactives/map-same-sex-criminalization/.

6. Associated Press, "Egypt's Gays Go Deeper Underground, Fearing Crackdown," December 19, 2014.

7. Andrew Buncombe, "India's Gay Community Scrambling After Court Decision Recriminalises Homosexuality," *Independent*, February 23, 2014, http://www.independent.co.uk/news/world/asia/indias-gay-community-scrambling-after-court-decision-recriminalises-homosexuality-9146244.html.

8. Drazen Jorgic, "Museveni Says He Plans to Sign Anti-Gay Law After All," Reuters, February 14, 2014. The article refers to the notorious Ugandan law, which, the article notes, "initially proposed a death sen-

tence for homosexual acts, but was amended to prescribe jail terms . . . for what it called aggravated homosexuality."

9. Adam Nossiter, "Wielding Whip and a Hard New Law, Nigeria Tries to 'Sanitize' Itself of Gays," *New York Times*, February 8, 2014.

10. Adam Nossiter, "Mob Attacks More Than a Dozen Gay Men in Nigeria's Capital," *New York Times*, February 16, 2014.

11. Marc Lacey and Laurie Goodstein, "African Anglican Leaders Outraged Over Gay Bishop in U.S.," *New York Times*, November 4, 2003.

12. *Lesbian, Gay, Bisexual, Transgender, Queer and HIV-Affected Hate Violence in 2012* (New York: National Coalition of Anti-Violence Programs, 2013). NCAVP notes that because its findings are based on reports made by victims and survivors to the local organizations that are members of the coalition, it is unlikely that these numbers reflect all incidents of violence against LGBTQ and HIV-affected people in the United States.

13. Ibid.

14. *Lynching in America: Confronting the Legacy of Racial Terror* (Montgomery, AL: Equal Justice Initiative, 2015). The report summary can be found at http://www.eji.org/files/EJI%20Lynching%20in%20America%20 SUMMARY.pdf.

15. Ibid., 6.

16. Initial efforts to combat lynching were led by African Americans who stepped into places of enormous risk in order to call public attention to the epidemic of lynching, protect those who had been targeted, and demand that perpetrators be brought to justice.

17. Walter White of the NAACP accused Southern evangelical Protestantism of being complicit in lynching in his searingly titled study *Rope and Faggot: A Biography of Judge Lynch* (Notre Dame, IN: University of Notre Dame Press, 2002). Jessie Daniel Ames, founder of the Association of Southern Women for the Prevention of Lynching, shared his concern and launched an investigation into possible connections between church revivals and lynchings. Ames's findings were never publicized, but Rachel McBride Lindsey notes that Ames saw the religious problem clearly: "On the one hand, religion was approached as the framework from which to condemn and eliminate lynching and, on the other, it was understood to generate and sustain the racialized animus that lynching manifested." "This Barbarous Practice: Southern Churchwomen and Race in the Association of Southern Women for the Prevention of Lynching, 1930–1942," *Journal of Southern Religion* 16 (2014).

18. Equal Justice Initiative, *Lynching in America*, 7. In "This Barbarous Practice," Lindsey explores the complex interplay of race and gender and of politics and religion at work in the activism to end lynching. She notes that most of the white women involved in this campaign held fast to "conservative theological anthropologies": "What is clear is that the Association, like other cultural arenas in the 1930s, was invested in the

racialized designation of 'white' Americans as much as 'the Negro.'" Reluctance to address deeper theological issues, or to appear political, had a significant impact on the movement: the association, fearing schism in its ranks, declined to support federal antilynching legislation.

19. Romans 5:5.
20. Barack Obama, "Remarks by the President in Eulogy for the Honorable Reverend Clementa Pinckney," College of Charleston, Charleston, SC, June 26, 2015.
21. Lizette Alvarez, "Families Hope Words Endure Past Shooting," *New York Times*, June 25, 2015.
22. I do not in any way mean to disregard the very real dangers that many people face in coming out. The challenge is especially acute for people who do not yet have a community of support, due to isolation of one kind or another. I will take this up—and discuss the imperative of safety planning—in chapter 8.
23. John 2:1–11.
24. I specify "gay friendly" here rather than "queer friendly" because while growing numbers of churches are developing comfort in recognizing gay and lesbian congregants and clergy, embracing others in the queer pantheon, including trans* individuals, lags behind, as does comfort with the word "queer" itself.
25. Romans 4:21–22.
26. Gen. 22:1–14.
27. Walter Brueggemann, *Genesis: Interpretation: A Bible Commentary for Teaching and Preaching* (Louisville, KY: Westminster John Knox Press, 1982).
28. The original quote is attributed to Theodore Parker, a nineteenth-century Unitarian minister, but it was frequently paraphrased and thus popularized by Martin Luther King Jr., including in his essay "Out of the Long Night," *Gospel Messenger*, a publication of the Church of the Brethren, February 8, 1958.

Chapter 4: Touch

1. See Audre Lorde, *Uses of the Erotic: The Erotic as Power* (Tucson: Kore Press, 1981).
2. 2 Cor. 11:2.
3. Thanks to Michael Bacon for his gnostic and queer insight into the bridal chamber.
4. Biblical scholar and bishop N. T. Wright, for example, offers an artful deconstruction of dualism in his paper "Mind, Spirit, Soul and Body: All for One and One for All: Reflections on Paul's Anthropology in His Complex Contexts," presented at the Society of Christian Philosophers Regional Meeting, Fordham University, New York, NY, March 18, 2011.

5. See, for example, Mark 1:40–45, KJV.
6. Isa. 6:1–9.
7. 1 John 4:18–20.

Chapter 5: Scandal

1. In *The Shawshank Redemption*, Red says this exact same sentence in response to Andy's proclamation about hope. It would appear that Miss Claudette is quoting him.
2. *Oxford English Dictionary*, s.v. "scandal," http://www.oxforddictionaries .com/us/definition/american_english/scandal.
3. Gerhard Friedrich, ed., *Theological Dictionary of the New Testament* (Grand Rapids, MI: Wm. B. Eerdmans, 1971), 7:339–58, s.v. "skandalon."
4. Michael Warner, *The Trouble with Normal: Sex, Politics, and the Ethics of Queer Life* (New York: Free Press, 1999), 34.
5. Ibid., 35.
6. Ibid. Emphasis mine.
7. Matt. 16:21–23.
8. Matt. 16:18–19.
9. Matt. 26:31–35.
10. 1 Cor. 1:18, 22–24.
11. Patrick S. Cheng, *From Sin to Amazing Grace: Discovering the Queer Christ* (New York: Seabury, 2012), 118.

Chapter 6: Adoption

1. L. E. Durso and G. J. Gates, *Serving Our Youth: Findings from a National Survey of Service Providers Working with Lesbian, Gay, Bisexual and Transgender Youth Who Are Homeless or at Risk of Becoming Homeless* (Los Angeles: The Williams Institute and True Colors Fund and The Palette Fund, 2012).
2. Queer activists in the United States have been working for decades to pass a federal Employment Non-Discrimination Act (ENDA). As originally drafted, ENDA would have barred employers with more than fifteen employees from discriminating in hiring and employment based on sexual orientation. "Gender identity" was added to the bill as a protected status in 2007; however, because of fear that the bill would not pass as written, "gender identity" was removed. Many queer activists were outraged by what was seen as an abandonment of trans* members of the LGBTQ community. The stripped-down bill did pass in the House of Representatives but failed to pass in the Senate. A trans*-inclusive bill was reintroduced by Rep. Barney Frank (D–MA) and by Sen. Jeff Merkley (D–OR) in 2011. The bill passed in the Senate in 2013 with bipartisan support, but as of 2015 had not passed in the House of Representatives.

3. Acts 9:1–19.

4. Isa. 42:6.

5. Brigitte Kahl's *Galatians Re-Imagined: Reading with the Eyes of the Vanquished* (Minneapolis: Fortress Press, 2010) has profound implications for many of the vexing issues that hamper progressive Christian engagement with Paul. Her commentary on Galatians is essential reading for exegetes, pastors, and preachers seeking to understand how the impulse to rupture binaries is embedded in the Christian tradition, and how and why it was forgotten by the church.

6. Gal. 3:28–29, 4:4b–7.

7. Kahl, *Galatians Re-Imagined*, 10–11.

8. Kahl's argument is informed by J. Louis Martyn's deconstruction of antinomies in *Galatians: A New Translation with Introduction and Commentary*, Anchor Bible 33A (New York: Doubleday, 1997). See Kahl's discussion of Martyn's work in *Galatians Re-Imagined*, 19–21.

9. Matt. 13:44.

Chapter 7: Pride

1. Charles M. Blow, "Up from Pain," *New York Times*, September 21, 2014. Adapted from *Fire Shut Up in My Bones* (New York: Houghton Mifflin Harcourt, 2014).

2. Cheng, *From Sin to Amazing Grace*, 118.

3. From here on out I'm going to use "Pride" with a capital "P" to signify queer Pride and, by extension, a kind of self-valuing that is healthy. I'm going to use "pride" with a lowercase "p" to signify conventional definitions of pride as spiritually problematic self-aggrandizement and hubris.

4. For a discussion of "religion as an optional extra," see Alison Webster, *Found Wanting: Women, Christianity and Sexuality* (London: Casell, 1995), 164, and Elizabeth Stuart, *Religion Is a Queer Thing: A Guide to the Christian Faith for Lesbian, Gay, Bisexual and Transgendered People* (Cleveland: Pilgrim Press, 1998), 14–15.

5. Valerie Saiving, "The Human Situation: A Feminine View," in *Womanspirit Rising*, ed. Carol P. Christ and Judith Plaskow (San Francisco: Harper & Row, 1979), 25–42.

6. Judith Plaskow, *Sex, Sin, and Grace: Women's Experience and the Theologies of Reinhold Niebuhr and Paul Tillich* (Washington, DC: University Press of America, 1980).

7. Gen. 22:1.

8. Exod. 3:4.

9. 1 Sam. 3:4.

10. Luke 1:38.

11. For example, the Episcopal Church (US) has commissioned the Task Force on the Study of Marriage, which is encouraging church-wide conversations. It has also issued a guide: Brian C. Taylor, ed., *Dearly Beloved:*

A Tool-kit for the Study of Marriage (New York: Episcopal Church, June 20, 2014), which can be found at https://extranet.generalconvention.org/staff/files/download/10613.

12. Lisa Isherwood and Marcella Althaus-Reid, "Introduction: Queering Theology," in *The Sexual Theologian: Essays on Sex, God, and Politics*, ed. Lisa Isherwood and Marcella Althaus-Reid (London: T & T Clark, 2004), 3.

13. Ibid.

Chapter 8: Coming Out

1. I use the word "homosexuality" intentionally, referring to public discourse that treats LGBTQ justice as an issue about which one can freely opine, rather than as a matter that concerns, first and foremost, the lives of real human beings.

2. For contact info at AVP, including the hotline number and a list of other US and Canadian organizations that work to reduce violence against LGBTQ people, go to www.avp.org.

3. Luke 24:48.

4. Elizabeth Stuart, "Why Bother with Christianity Anyway?" in *Religion Is a Queer Thing: A Guide to the Christian Faith for Lesbian, Gay, Bisexual and Transgendered People* (Cleveland: Pilgrim Press, 1997), 15.

5. Walter Brueggemann, *The Prophetic Imagination*, 2nd ed. (Minneapolis: Fortress Press, 2001), xvi.

6. There is an interesting and robust conversation taking place among young evangelical Christians about what it means to be countercultural in today's world. See, for example, Laura Turner, "The Trouble with Being Counter Cultural," *Entertaining Faith* (blog), February 5, 2015, http://lauraturner.religionnews.com/2015/02/05/trouble-counter-cul tural/#comments; and Matthew Lee Anderson, "Writing as Though History Happened: On Being Countercultural Christians," *Mere Orthodoxy* (blog), February 10, 2015, http://mereorthodoxy.com/writing -though-history-happened-countercultural-christians/.

7. Michael Paulson, "Church Is Now More Informal, Study Finds," *New York Times*, September 12, 2014.

8. Walter Brueggemann, *The Practice of Prophetic Imagination: Preaching an Emancipating Word* (Minneapolis: Fortress Press, 2012), 45.

9. Michael Eric Dyson, "Racial Terror, Fast and Slow," *New York Times*, April 17, 2015.

Chapter 9: Authenticity

1. Sean Yoong Putrajaya, "Malaysia Marks National Day," *China Post*, September 1, 2003.

2. Patrick S. Cheng, *Radical Love: An Introduction to Queer Theology* (Seabury Books, 2011), 74–75.

3. Nossiter, "Wielding Whip."

4. Davis Mac-Iyalla, "Unite to Condemn Homophobic Laws: An Open Letter to the Archbishop of Canterbury and Primates of the Anglican Communion on Uganda's Anti-Homosexuality Bill," *Guardian* (UK), November 10, 2009.

5. Jenn Cruickshank, "Out of the Ashes: Grief, Conflict, and Growing in Love in a Community of Faith" (working paper, New College University of Edinburgh, 2010). Per standard practice following a clergy departure, I had no contact with Jenn or the other students at Canterbury for several years. Four years after I left, Jenn reached out to me and sent this paper as a gesture of good faith, and good intention.

6. John 13:35.

7. Thanks to Caroline Perry for her insight into this dynamic.

8. To be clear, the Canterbury community includes its board of directors and exists within the larger community of a diocese. It would not have been appropriate for me to process this issue with the undergraduates in my ministry, but it would have been both appropriate and wise to bring it to my bishop and to my board of directors sooner than I eventually did.

9. 1 Cor. 12:14–15, 18–21.

10. For example, the African Methodist Episcopal Church was founded by Richard Allen and other African Americans in 1787 after white members of a Methodist church in Philadelphia forcibly segregated black worshippers. Allen's friend and colleague Absalom Jones went on to become the first African American ordained in the Episcopal Church. Rather than building a new denomination, Jones wanted to establish a congregation that would be governed by its black members while remaining inside the Episcopal Church. The African Episcopal Church of St. Thomas, founded by Jones in 1794, is still active in Philadelphia.

Chapter 10: Hospitality

1. Elizabeth Stuart, "Sex in Heaven," in *Sex These Days: Essays on Theology, Sexuality and Society*, ed. Jon Davies and Gerard Loughlin (Sheffield, UK: Sheffield Academic Press, 1997), 195.

2. Rev. 1:4.

3. Jürgen Moltmann, "Theology as Eschatology," in *The Future of Hope: Theology as Eschatology*, ed. Frederick Herzog (New York: Herder & Herder, 1970), 11.

4. Exod. 3:7.

5. "Dreamers" refers to young people who have advocated for both federal and state iterations of the Dream Act, legislation that would allow undocumented students to receive financial aid for higher education.

6. José Esteban Muñoz was a queer theorist who, like Moltmann, was influenced by Ernst Bloch's philosophy of hope. Where Moltmann sees

the future as a modality of God, Muñoz argues that "the future is queerness's domain." His book *Cruising Utopia: The Then and There of Queer Futurity* explores eschatological themes running through queer political movements and literature. Articulating his own eschatological vision, Muñoz posits a rupturing in which "we must strive, in the face of the here and now's totalizing rendering of reality, to think and feel a *then and there*." Pursuing queerness, he writes, calls us to "dream and enact new and better pleasures, other ways of being in the world, and ultimately new worlds." *Cruising Utopia* (New York: New York University Press, 2009), 1.

Conclusion

1. Winnie Varghese, Palm Sunday sermon, St. Mark's in the Bowery, New York, NY, April 13, 2014, http://stmarksbowery.org/welcome/sermons/palm-sunday/.